Oxford *Smart*

QUEST

ENGLISH LANGUAGE AND LITERATURE

2

Paul Clayton

Ramender Crompton

Lance Hanson

CW01401534

OXFORD
UNIVERSITY PRESS

Contents

Welcome to Quest!

Quest delivers the 11–14 segment of the Oxford Smart Curriculum Service for English and has been written to:

- build on the variety of learner experiences at KS2 and explore English as a unique discipline, empowering, engaging and motivating both learners and teachers

- support teachers in delivering a diverse, relevant and challenging curriculum

- look back across the rich literary heritage of English Literature but also forwards to a future dominated by the digital world

- allow teachers to identify and address misconceptions and misunderstandings

- provide access to high-quality texts from a wide range of writers, both classic and contemporary, and from a range of backgrounds, cultures and experiences

- offer flexibility and choice while still delivering the core skills and knowledge so that teachers can customise their route through the resources

- enable efficient and effective progress tracking, giving teachers the confidence that students will be ready to embark on their GCSE studies by the end of Year 9.

Course overview

Student Books

Quest includes digital and printed Student Books for each year of KS3. Book 1 builds on the knowledge students have from KS2 and introduces them to a wide variety of texts and themes, while laying the foundation for future English study. Books 2 and 3 develop students' knowledge and skills further and prepare them for English at KS4.

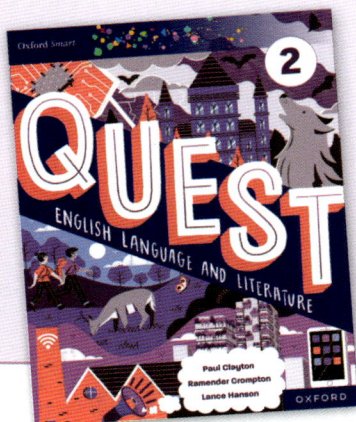

Teacher Books

Digital and printed Teacher Books help support the planning and implementation of Quest. Each of the three Teacher Books contains introductions to the Student Book topics, flexible lesson plans with unit-by-unit guidance, additional activity ideas, assessment support, further reading suggestions, plus tips on how to integrate the Kerboodle resources into your lessons.

Kerboodle

Oxford Smart Quest Kerboodle provides access to digital versions of the Student Books and Teacher Books, additional teaching and learning resources, as well as a comprehensive assessment package. Resources include worksheets with alternative texts, audio recordings of source texts, answers to Student Book activities, automatically marked assessments, as well as a CPD and Research Hub that includes a wealth of resources to support your professional development.

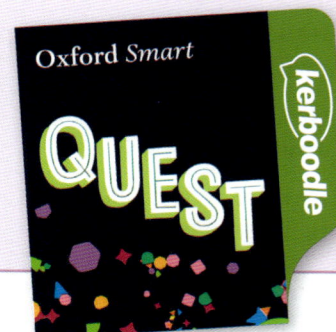

Using the Quest Student Book

In each chapter

Chapter opener: Each chapter in the Student Book starts with a chapter opener that activates prior knowledge and informs students about what they will be learning.

Learning overview: The learning overview supports metacognition by preparing students for what they will be learning and will help them to monitor what they have learned. It also shows a coherent learning pathway through the Student Book.

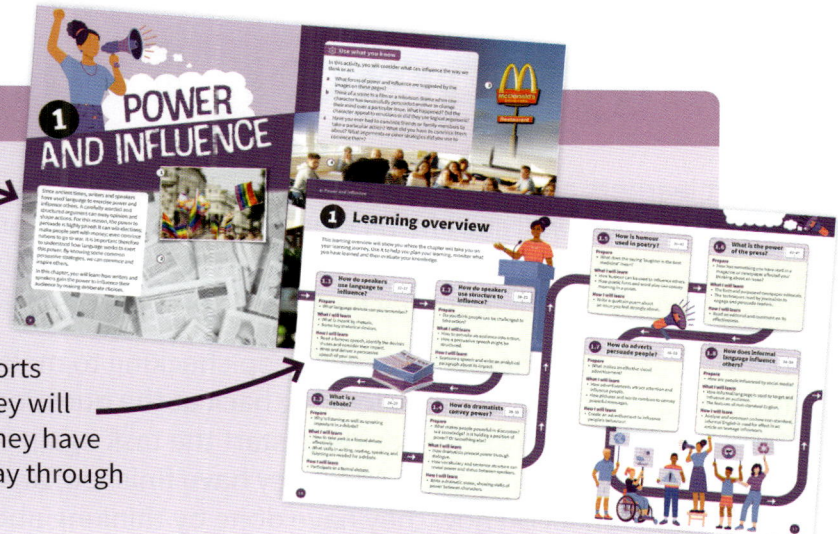

In each unit

Learning objectives focus on what students will be learning and how they will demonstrate their understanding. The first objective is about what the student will learn, the second is about what they are exploring, investigating or considering further and the third objective is to write, analyse or present what they have learned.

What's the big idea? gives an overview of what the unit is about and why it is important. It can also include links to previous units as a reminder of what students already know.

⭐ Boosting your vocabulary

Boosting your vocabulary sections provide activities and strategies to help students work out unfamiliar Tier 2 words from the source texts, along with opportunities for them to practise using the words in their own writing.

💡 Building your knowledge

Building your knowledge sections introduce the knowledge focus of each unit in the context of the source text. Students are encouraged to think about what they already know and understand about the focus of the unit, drawing on their own experiences.

🧩 Putting it all together

Putting it all together sections conclude each unit. The tasks in the unit build towards students completing a final activity that will allow them to demonstrate that they can apply the skills and knowledge covered.

Features

✅ **Tips** remind students of a connection to another key piece of knowledge or key skill and give prompts.

❓ **Did you know?** offers short and snappy facts to aid or add to students' comprehension of a text.

🗝 **Key terms** are flagged the first time they appear in a chapter and include technical or literary terms. A complete glossary of key terms is included at the end of each Student Book.

⬆ **Stretch yourself** activities encourage students to think in more depth or to take their learning further in order to expand their knowledge and develop their skills.

✏ **Writing icons** indicate when students are expected to write their answer or response to the activity.

Plan, Monitor, Evaluate

Expert learners approach new and unfamiliar tasks in a structured way. Often, they will start by picking apart the question or task, thinking carefully about what subject knowledge or skill they are going to need or whether they have seen something similar before.

During a task an expert learner will keep checking to make sure they are on track by regularly looking back at the question. Sometimes they may even decide to start the task again and choose a different approach. After they have finished, an expert learner will reflect on how they have done by thinking about any areas of improvement and putting a plan together for what they would do differently next time.

The Plan, Monitor, Evaluate cycle is a structure you can follow to help you approach a new task like an expert learner. This cycle should be used every time you complete a task.

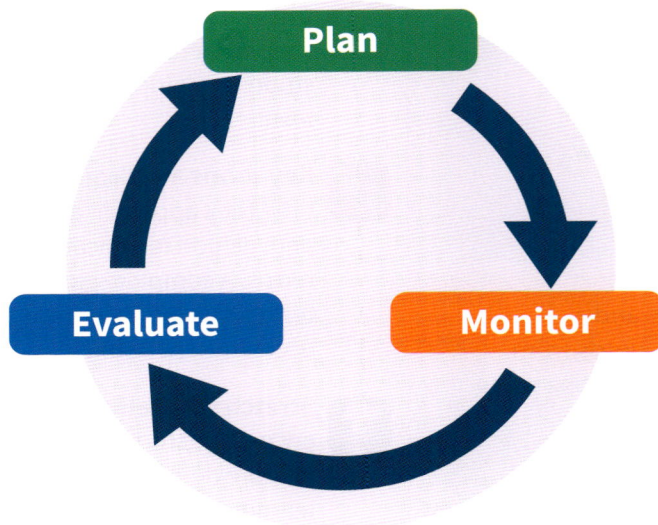

Activity

Discuss your answers to these questions:

a   When does the planning phase take place?

b   How can you monitor your progress during the monitoring phase?

c   Why is the evaluation phase important?

Plan

The planning phase takes place **before** you start the task. This is where you plan your approach to the task by thinking about what you already know and what pieces of information relate to the task.

Here are some examples of the types of questions you could be asking yourself before you start a new task.

- How many marks does this question have?
- What knowledge or skill do I need to recall to answer the question?
- Have I answered a similar question before? What did success look like then?
- What have I learnt from the examples my teacher has shown me?

Evaluate

When you have completed a task, it is important to reflect on how you have done. An expert learner learns from their mistakes and uses teacher feedback to move their own learning forward.

Here are some examples of the types of questions you should be asking yourself after a task.

- What went well?
- Did I miss any marks? If so, for what?
- Is there any other strategy that I could have used to complete this task?
- What areas do I need to improve upon for next time?

Monitor

Once you have started the task it is important to monitor your own progress. Sometimes by pausing and reviewing the task you may choose to change your approach. You may even decide that you need to go back and re-read some content to help you complete the task.

Here are some examples of the types of questions you should be asking yourself during a task.

- How do I feel now that I am answering the question? Confident or unsure?
- Am I meeting the requirements of the task or question?
- Do I need to stop and change anything I have done?
- Have I followed the examples that my teacher has shown me?

1 POWER AND INFLUENCE

Since ancient times, writers and speakers have used language to exercise power and influence others. A carefully worded and structured argument can sway opinion and shape actions. For this reason, the power to persuade is highly prized: it can win elections; make people part with money; even convince nations to go to war. It is important therefore to understand how language works to exert this power. By knowing some common persuasive strategies, we can convince and inspire others.

In this chapter, you will learn how writers and speakers gain the power to influence their audience by making deliberate choices.

⚙ Use what you know

In this activity, you will consider what can influence the way we think or act.

a What forms of power and influence are suggested by the images on these pages?

b Think of a scene in a film or a television drama when one character has successfully persuaded another to change their mind over a particular issue. What happened? Did the character appeal to emotions or did they use logical argument?

c Have you ever had to convince friends or family members to take a particular action? What did you have to convince them about? What arguments or other strategies did you use to convince them?

3

4

Words you need to know

argument, debate, persuasion, rhetoric, dramatist, journalist, activist, influencer

5

6

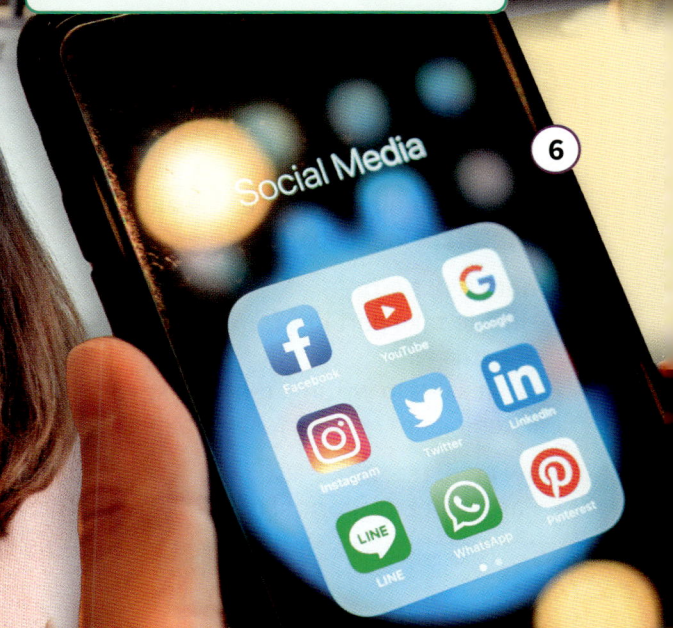

1 Learning overview

This learning overview will show you where the chapter will take you on your learning journey. Use it to help you plan your learning, monitor what you have learned and then evaluate your knowledge.

1.1 How do speakers use language to influence?
12–17

Prepare
- What language devices can you remember?

What I will learn
- What is meant by rhetoric.
- Some key rhetorical devices.

How I will learn
- Read a famous speech, identify the devices it uses and consider their impact.
- Write and deliver a persuasive speech of your own.

1.2 How do speakers use structure to influence?
18–23

Prepare
- Do you think people can be challenged to take action?

What I will learn
- How to provoke an audience into action.
- How a persuasive speech might be structured.

How I will learn
- Examine a speech and write an analytical paragraph about its impact.

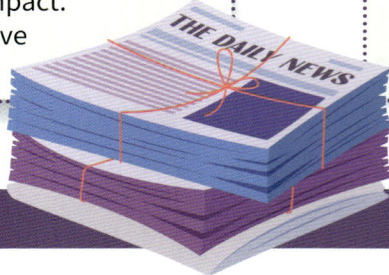

1.3 What is a debate?
24–29

Prepare
- Why is listening as well as speaking important in a debate?

What I will learn
- How to take part in a formal debate effectively.
- What skills in writing, reading, speaking and listening are needed for a debate.

How I will learn
- Participate in a formal debate.

1.4 How do dramatists convey power?
30–35

Prepare
- What makes people powerful in discussion? Is it knowledge? Is it holding a position of power? Or something else?

What I will learn
- How dramatists present power through dialogue.
- How vocabulary and sentence structure can reveal power and status between speakers.

How I will learn
- Write a dramatic scene, showing shifts of power between characters.

1.5 How is humour used in poetry?
36–41

Prepare
- What does the saying 'laughter is the best medicine' mean?

What I will learn
- How humour can be used to influence others.
- How poetic form and word play can convey meaning in a poem.

How I will learn
- Write a quatrain poem about an issue you feel strongly about.

1.6 What is the power of the press?
42–47

Prepare
- How has something you have read in a magazine or newspaper affected your thinking about an issue?

What I will learn
- The form and purpose of newspaper editorials.
- The techniques used by journalists to engage and persuade readers.

How I will learn
- Read an editorial and comment on its effectiveness.

1.7 How do adverts persuade people?
48–53

Prepare
- What makes an effective visual advertisement?

What I will learn
- How advertisements attract attention and influence people.
- How pictures and words combine to convey powerful messages.

How I will learn
- Create an advertisement to influence people's behaviour.

1.8 How does informal language influence others?
54–59

Prepare
- How are people influenced by social media?

What I will learn
- How informal language is used to target and influence an audience.
- The features of non-standard English.

How I will learn
- Analyse and comment on how non-standard, informal English is used for effect in an article on teenage influencers.

1.1 How do speakers use language to influence?

In this unit, you will:

- learn what is meant by rhetoric
- explore some key rhetorical devices
- use these devices to write and deliver a persuasive speech.

What's the big idea?

For thousands of years, people have sought to resolve conflicts, uncover truths, and reconcile differences of opinion through argument. People who use language skilfully in arguments have power to influence others, to persuade them to see a particular perspective. We call this skill with language rhetoric.

In this unit, you will read a famous speech that uses many well-known rhetorical devices. Then you will use what you have learned to write and present a speech of your own.

⚙ Activity 1

a   There is a saying: 'It's not what you say, it's how you say it.' Look at the quotations below. The ones in column A have a similar meaning to those in column B. Discuss which version sounds more impressive or memorable.

Column A	Column B
'the stuttering rifles' rapid rattle'	'the uncertain fast gun sound'
'I came, I saw, I conquered.'	'I arrived and looked about a bit. Then I won a few battles.'
'It was the best of times, it was the worst of times.'	'It was not only a really good moment, but also a terrible phase too.'
'If you prick us, do we not bleed?'	'We bleed when you prick us.'

b   Explain the reasons for your choices. Do the quotations use any literary or **rhetorical devices** that you already know about?

🔑 Key term

rhetorical device
a language feature that has a persuasive or impressive effect on listeners and readers

The following speech was delivered by Barack Obama on becoming the first Black President of the United States. Obama wanted to inspire his audience and persuade his listeners that they could overcome any challenges that they might face. In this extract, he refers to a particular voter Ann Nixon Cooper, who was 106 years old.

Extract from President Obama's victory speech, 4 November 2008

She was born just a generation past slavery; a time when there were no cars on the road or planes in the sky; when someone like her couldn't vote for two reasons – because she was a woman and because of the colour of her skin.

And tonight, I think about all that she's seen throughout her century in America – the heartache
5 and the hope; the struggle and the progress; the times we were told that we can't, and the people who pressed on with that American creed: Yes we can.

At a time when women's voices were silenced and their hopes dismissed, she lived to see them stand up and speak out and reach for the **ballot**. Yes we can.

When there was despair in the **dust bowl** and **depression** across the land, she saw a nation
10 conquer fear itself with a **New Deal**, new jobs, a new sense of common purpose. Yes we can.

When the bombs fell on our **Harbor** and tyranny threatened the world, she was there to witness a generation rise to greatness and a democracy was saved. Yes we can. [...]

And this year, in this election, she touched her finger to a screen, and cast her vote, because after 106 years in America, through the best of times and the darkest of hours, she knows how America
15 can change. Yes we can.

America, we have come so far. We have seen so much. But there is so much more to do. So tonight, let us ask ourselves – if our children should live to see the next century; if my daughters should be so lucky to live as long as Ann Nixon Cooper, what change will they see? What progress will we have made?

20 This is our chance to answer that call. This is our moment. This is our time, to put our people back to work and open doors of opportunity for our kids; to restore prosperity and promote the cause of peace; to reclaim the American dream and reaffirm that fundamental truth, that, out of many, we are one; that while we breathe, we hope.

And where we are met with cynicism and doubts and those who tell us that we can't, we will
25 respond with that timeless creed that sums up the spirit of a people: Yes, we can.

---

ballot – the system of voting
dust bowl – land which has become dust because of drought; also the name given to a period of drought in 1930s America
depression – a time of mass unemployment in America during the 1930s
New Deal – a set of government measures in America to improve the economy and create jobs
Harbor – Pearl Harbor was attacked by Japanese forces in December 1941, provoking America to join the Second World War

⭐ Boosting your vocabulary

Skilled speakers choose their words with care. The activity below explores some of the vocabulary used in the source text, which has been highlighted on page 13.

Activity 2

Looking at the **etymology** of a word can often help our understanding of a whole group of words.

a   The word 'creed' means belief. It comes from the Latin word *credo* meaning 'I believe'. Many modern words are related to 'creed' and contain the **root** 'cred'. For example, 'credulous' means a willingness to believe in things too quickly. What other words can you think of that contain the root 'cred' and link to the idea of belief?

b   Find the words below in Obama's speech and match them to the correct definition. Use the context of the speech to help you.

Words	Definitions
generation	financial success
progress	a society which is governed by people chosen by the population
democracy	forward movement towards a better position
prosperity	all the people who were born at about the same time

✏ c   Write two sentences correctly using two of the words above. Consider the definitions and meanings of the words as you write your sentences.

> ✅ **Tip**
>
> Remember the root can appear anywhere in the word: at the beginning, middle or end of the word.

> 🔑 **Key terms**
>
> **etymology** a description of the origin and history of a particular word
>
> **root** the core of a word that has meaning. It may or may not be a complete word

Building your knowledge

Obama's speech contains many rhetorical devices, which have been used to help make his message memorable and to persuade his audience to agree with his point of view. Many of these rhetorical devices have been used by writers and speakers for thousands of years.

Activity 3

Look at the rhetorical devices listed in the table below and read their definitions.

Rhetorical device	Definition
alliteration	using the same sound at the beginning of several words for special effect, e.g. *the wild west wind*
parallelism	closely repeating the grammatical structure of a phrase or sentence, e.g. *The game was long, the team was tired, the result was disappointing*
tricolon	a pattern of three words, phrases or sentences grouped for effect, e.g. *The resort promised sun, sand and sea*
rhetorical question	a question not intended to be answered but used for dramatic effect, e.g. *Isn't it true that everyone likes this film?*

a   Identify which of the rhetorical devices above is used in each of the following quotations taken from Obama's speech:

'there were no cars on the road or planes in the sky'

'What progress will we have made?'

'she lived to see them stand up and speak out and reach for the ballot'

'the heartache and the hope'

b   Write two sentences of your own that use two of the rhetorical devices listed above. Consider the impact that the rhetorical device has.

Stretch yourself

Identify two other rhetorical devices that are used in Obama's speech.

Did you know?

Enheduanna, an astronomer and priestess who lived over 4,000 years ago and who is generally recognised as the earliest known named author, used many of these rhetorical devices.

The Ancient Greek philosopher Aristotle said that a successful persuasive speech needs three core elements:

> **1 Logical argument** *(logos)*
> This means something that can be proved by facts, statistics, reason and research. For example, regular exercise improves health and well-being; this is a truth that is supported by research.

Activity 4

Re-read lines 1–3 of Obama's speech. List the things that he mentions that can be proven to be factually true.

> **2 An appeal to the emotions** *(pathos)*
> **Emotive language** that provokes feelings such as fear, envy or sympathy can increase the impact of the words. For example, 'an inferno' sounds more powerful than 'a fire'; 'prices slashed' is more dramatic than 'prices reduced'.

Activity 5

a Re-read lines 4–8 and list all the emotive words and phrases you can find.

b Look at the pairs of sentences below. Which sentence in each pair uses the more emotive language?

i	The man shouted.	The man yelled.
ii	The woman was frozen.	The woman was cold.
iii	The day was magical.	The day was enjoyable.
iv	They ran for help.	They dashed for help.

> **3 A trustworthy speaker** *(ethos)*
> We are generally more likely to be persuaded by someone who we feel we can trust and like, than by a speaker who we feel is dishonest. A reference or **anecdote** about friends or family adds a personal feel to a speech.

🔑 Key terms

anecdote a short or entertaining story about real people or events

emotive language word choices that create a strong emotional reaction in the audience or reader

Activity 6

Re-read lines 16–25. What do they suggest about the speaker's character? What things does he seem to value? Try to express your ideas in the following way:

The speaker values family. This is shown when he refers to his own daughters.

Putting it all together

Activity 7

Write a persuasive speech, using the skills and knowledge you have explored in this unit. Remember that an effective, persuasive speech combines facts with emotional appeal and expresses ideas and opinions using a range of rhetorical devices.

a Choose one of the topics below or one of your own.
  • Persuade the members of your class to watch a particular television programme.
  • Persuade the Head Teacher to introduce a shorter school day.
  • Persuade the school governors to hold an end-of-term celebration.

b Remind yourself of the three core elements on page 16 used to create a powerful speech. Then plan your speech carefully, following the steps below.

> **Paragraph 1:** Explain what you intend to persuade the audience to do.
>
> ↓
>
> **Paragraph 2:** Give some personal information or an anecdote that says why you believe what you do. This should encourage the audience to trust you.
>
> ↓
>
> **Paragraph 3:** Offer some facts and statistics that support your point of view.
>
> ↓
>
> **Paragraph 4:** Acknowledge that not everyone shares your views and give some reasons why they might think differently.
>
> ↓
>
> **Paragraph 5:** Address their concerns.
>
> ↓
>
> **Paragraph 6:** Finish by restating your viewpoint.

c Before presenting your speech, rehearse it aloud. If there are places which do not flow properly, or which seem unclear, you may want to edit your speech. Shorter, simpler sentences are sometimes more effective than long, complex sentences in a speech.

1.2 How do speakers use structure to influence?

In this unit, you will:

- learn how to provoke your audience into action
- explore structural techniques in a persuasive speech
- analyse the impact of a persuasive speech.

What's the big idea?

In the last unit, you looked at how speakers use rhetorical devices to convey their ideas persuasively and effectively to an audience. The way a speech is structured can also be used to provoke an audience, stirring them to take action. These persuasive techniques can give the speaker power and influence over their listeners.

In this unit, you will look at a speech by the climate activist Greta Thunberg that is structured in a way that deliberately seeks to rouse her audience to take action.

Activity 1

a What strategies could you use in a persuasive speech to provoke your audience into action? Think about the rhetorical techniques covered in Unit 1. Consider the reaction you might want to create and how you might achieve this.

b In his book *The 48 Laws of Power*, Robert Greene uses **epigrams** to explain how people use power to influence others. For example, his epigram 'Stir up waters to catch fish' suggests that sometimes you should provoke your listeners to achieve your aims. Link each epigram below to its meaning.

Key term

epigram the expression of an idea in a short, memorable way

Epigrams	Meanings
Work on the hearts and minds of others.	If you take charge of a situation, you will be able to limit and control the potential outcomes.
Get others to play with the cards you deal.	Influence others by appealing to both their reason and their emotions.
Don't build fortresses to protect yourself.	Don't hide away; instead, influence others by being among them.

In 2019, Greta Thunberg was invited to speak to British Members of Parliament about her concerns for the future. As you read the following extract from her speech, think about what techniques she uses to try to provoke her listeners into action.

Extract from Greta Thunberg's speech to the UK Parliament, 23 April 2019

I was fortunate to be born in a time and place where everyone told us to dream big; I could become whatever I wanted to. I could live wherever I wanted to. People like me had
5 everything we needed and more. Things our grandparents could not even dream of. We had everything we could ever wish for and yet now we may have nothing.

Now we probably don't even have a future any
10 more.

Because that future was sold so that a small number of people could make unimaginable amounts of money. It was stolen from us every time you said that the sky was the limit,
15 and that you only live once.

You lied to us. You gave us false hope. You told us that the future was something to look forward to. And the saddest thing is that most children are not even aware of the fate
20 that awaits us. We will not understand it until it's too late. And yet we are the lucky ones. Those who will be affected the hardest are already suffering the consequences. But their voices are not heard.

25 The climate crisis is both the easiest and the hardest issue we have ever faced. The easiest because we know what we must do. We must stop the emissions of greenhouse gases. The hardest because our current economics are
30 still totally dependent on burning fossil fuels, and thereby destroying ecosystems in order to create everlasting economic growth.

"So, exactly how do we solve that?" you ask us – the schoolchildren **striking** for the climate.

35 And we say: "No one knows for sure. But we have to stop burning fossil fuels and restore nature and many other things that we may not have quite figured out yet."

Then you say: "That's not an answer!"

40 So we say: "We have to start treating the crisis like a crisis – and act even if we don't have all the solutions."

"That's still not an answer," you say.

Then we start talking about circular economy
45 and rewilding nature and the need for a just transition. Then you don't understand what we are talking about.

We say that all those solutions needed are not known to anyone and therefore we must unite
50 behind the science and find them together along the way. But you do not listen to that. Because those answers are for solving a crisis that most of you don't even fully understand. Or don't want to understand.

---

striking – refusing to do something (such as working or going to school) as a way of protesting

---

❓ Did you know?

Greta Thunberg has spoken all over the world about climate change. In 2019, aged 17, she was named by *Time* magazine as their 'Person of the Year'. A full version of the above speech by Greta Thunberg to the UK Parliament can be found in the Quest Kerboodle digital resources.

★ Boosting your vocabulary

Skilled speakers choose their words with care. In the speech, Thunberg says that her listeners 'do not understand what we are talking about' and uses specialist, technical language to communicate with her supporters.

Activity 2 focuses on this, then Activity 3 explores the vocabulary used in the source text, which has been highlighted on page 19.

Activity 2

a Select five technical words or phrases that Thunberg uses in her speech. Use the definitions below to help you identify relevant terms.

> networks of living things that depend on each other

> fuels such as coal and gas that have been formed over millions of years in the Earth's crust

> gases that form a layer in the Earth's atmosphere and trap the heat in. If too many of these gases are produced, the planet gets hotter and hotter

> returning an area of land to its natural, wild state

> a way of preserving the Earth's limited resources by recycling, sharing, reusing and repairing products for as long as possible

b What other technical language do you know that links with the topic of climate change, energy resources and the environment? Explain what your chosen words mean.

Activity 3

a Thunberg uses the term 'a just transition'. Decide which of the three meanings below is most accurate in the context of the speech. Give reasons for your choice.

> It is only a change.

> It is a change that can be justified.

> It is a change that makes things fairer.

b Write your own sentence using the word 'transition' correctly.

c The **prefix** 'trans-' comes from the Latin word *trans*, which means 'across'. What other words do you know that use this prefix to convey a similar idea? Explain how these words link to the idea of across or beyond.

> ## 🔑 Key term
>
> **prefix** a word or group of letters placed in front of another word to add to or change its meaning

Building your knowledge

Thunberg presents herself and her listeners as **antagonists**: like two people in an argument. The speech moves from one perspective to another. While Thunberg and her followers are presented as eager to stop climate change and protect the Earth for future generations, her listeners are presented as indifferent and unsupportive.

Thunberg reinforces this impression of division and contrast through her choice of language and structure in this speech. In the activities below, you will explore how this language of contrast is built up through **tone**, **pronouns** (including the use of **direct address**), **antithesis** (a rhetorical device that uses opposing ideas) and **direct speech**.

Activity 4

How would you describe the tone of Thunberg's speech? For example, is it friendly, humorous, playful or sad? Choose your own word to describe the tone and give reasons for your choice.

Activity 5

Read lines 1–24 of Thunberg's speech again, noticing her use of the pronouns 'I', 'we', 'us' and 'you'.

a   How does she portray herself and other teenagers?

b   In contrast, how does she use direct address to portray her listeners? Choose suitable words from the list below.

> treacherous   betrayed   dishonest   deceitful
>
> deceived   misleading   angry
>
> doomed   powerless   false

c   Explain and support your choices by quoting from her speech.

> **Tip**
>
> You may find it helpful to imagine how this speech might *sound* in order to describe the tone.

> **Key terms**
>
> **antagonist** main opponent
>
> **antithesis** a rhetorical device that expresses opposing or contrasting ideas
>
> **direct address** addressing the reader as you
>
> **direct speech** the words that are actually spoken, usually presented in quotation marks
>
> **pronoun** a word used instead of a noun or noun phrase, e.g. *he, it, they*
>
> **tone** the speaker's (or writer's) feeling or attitude expressed towards their subject

Thunberg uses antithesis in her speech by introducing two opposing words when describing the issue of climate change: 'the easiest and the hardest'. The effect of this contrast in the speech is to emphasise the conflicting ideas. These words are both also **superlatives** so take the point she is making to the extreme. She then builds on this point by explaining in the following two sentences *why* the issue is both 'the easiest' and 'the hardest'.

> 🗝 **Key term**
>
> **superlative** the form of an adjective or adverb that means 'most'

Activity 6

Read lines 25–32 of the speech where Thunberg explains why the issue is the easiest in one sentence and the hardest in the next.

a Notice how these two sentences differ in length. What is the effect of this? What does it make the reader think or imagine about the issue of climate change?

b How would the effect be different if the speaker adopted a different order: speaking about 'the hardest' first and then 'the easiest'?

c How would the effect be different if a short sentence was used to explain why it was the hardest issue to face, and a long sentence to explain why it was the easiest?

From line 33 onwards, Thunberg uses direct speech to present both her listeners' assumed responses and her own (which represent the views of 'the schoolchildren striking for the climate'). This builds up the effect that we are witnessing a dialogue – or a heated argument.

However, we never really get to hear her listeners' actual views; only Thunberg's version of what she believes they might think and say. This is to provoke a response from her audience: listeners might feel that Thunberg is not representing them fairly and therefore feel forced to respond.

Activity 7

Look at lines 33–43 in which Thunberg uses direct speech to structure her argument and answer the points that challenge it. How successful do you think this technique is to provoke an audience into action?

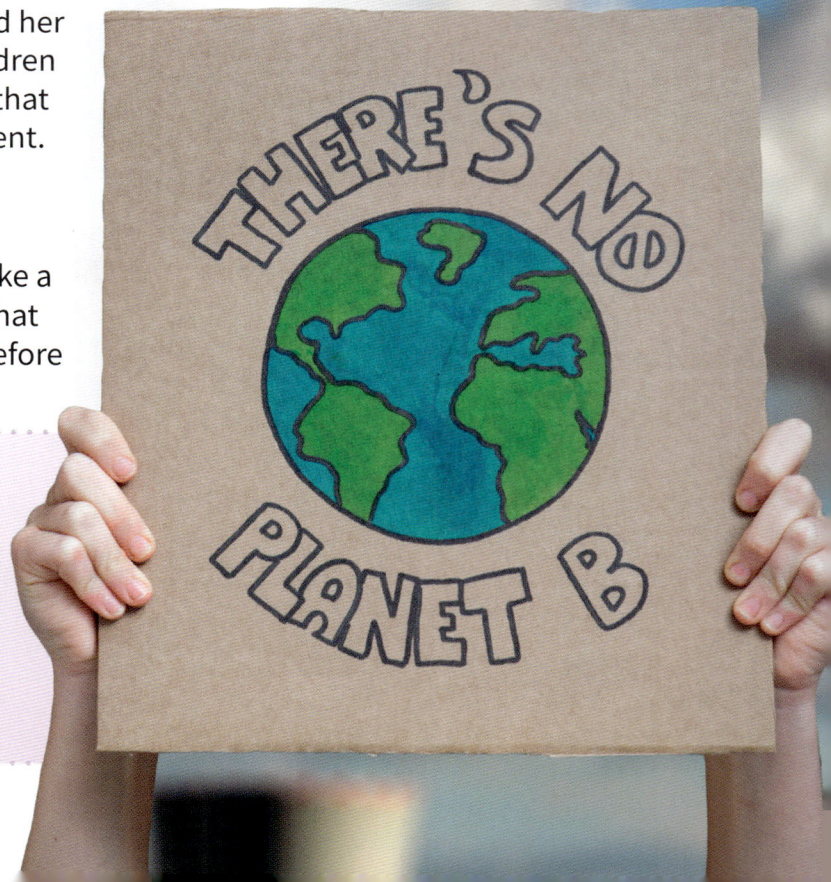

Putting it all together

In this unit, you have seen how Thunberg uses the idea of contrast to structure her speech, and language features to reinforce those contrasts. By suggesting that her listeners fail to understand the issues, Thunberg aims to provoke people into action. However, it could also be argued that her direct approach works against her and makes her audience more defensive.

Activity 8

Do you agree or disagree with the statement below? Write a paragraph explaining your view. Think carefully about the structural and language techniques you have explored in Activities 4–7.

> 'After listening to Greta Thunberg's speech, I think an audience would be persuaded to join her movement to fight climate change.'

Step 1: Look at the statements below. Select the ones you most agree with.

1 Thunberg's passionate tone would provoke her audience to take steps to fight climate change.	2 Thunberg's audience would be put off by her direct tone and become unsympathetic to her ideas.
3 The speech is carefully and effectively structured to lead her listeners to agree with her viewpoint.	4 The speech lacks a clear structure and therefore it is not clear what Thunberg wants her audience to do after they have heard it.
5 The speaker has chosen language carefully, for example using specialist terms to make it clear that she knows what she is talking about.	6 The speaker uses specialist terminology that would not be understood by her listeners.

Step 2: Put the statements that you have chosen in order of effectiveness, putting the most forceful one at the end.

Step 3: Use the statements to write your paragraph, remembering to quote from the text to support the statements that you use. Add any words and phrases necessary to link the statements so that your paragraph reads smoothly and fluently.

1.3 What is a debate?

In this unit, you will:

- learn how to take part in a formal debate effectively

- practise the writing, speaking and listening skills needed for a debate

- participate in a formal debate in the classroom.

What's the big idea?

People debate to explore issues where there are strongly opposing viewpoints. In a debate, everyone has an opportunity to contribute their thoughts and opinions, and to challenge others' ideas, in a fair and balanced way. At the end of a debate, a vote is taken to decide whose argument is the most convincing.

In the previous two units, you learned how a speaker can use rhetoric and structure to influence people, persuade them to share a point of view or stir them into action. In this unit, you will build on this by developing your knowledge of formal debating. You will learn how to discuss controversial issues and how to put forward your own views firmly and persuasively and then have the opportunity to use these skills in a formal class debate.

⚙ Activity 1

a   Draw up a Know, Find out and Learned (KFL) grid like the one below. In the first column, write all you *know* about debating. In the second column, write what you would like to *find out*. At the end of this unit, you will write down what you have *learned* in the third column.

Know	Find out	Learned
There are always two sides in a debate	What are the rules of debating?	

b   Rate your confidence in the following areas from 1 to 10 (with 10 being the most confident). Which area do you feel least confident in?

   i   speaking in front of class
   ii   listening carefully
   iii   responding to questions
   iv   constructing an argument
   v   creating counter-arguments

c   What will you do to improve your confidence in this area? At the end of this unit, you will revisit these areas.

Building your knowledge

A debate is based around a statement (called a **motion**). For example, '**This house believes** that teachers should be replaced by robots.' People in the debate would argue for or against the motion. The 'house' refers to everyone involved in the debate: the speakers that are on both sides.

People who agree with the statement are called 'speakers for the **proposition**'. Those who disagree are known as 'speakers for the **opposition**'.

A **chairperson** helps to control the debate, inviting people to speak and ensuring that everyone follows the rules.

A formal debate follows a set structure:

1 The chairperson introduces the debate and states the motion.

↓

2 The first proposition speaker puts forward reasons for agreeing with the motion.

↓

3 The first opposition speaker explains why the motion should be rejected.

↓

4 Other speakers from both sides take it in turns to present their arguments or offer alternative viewpoints.

↓

5 Questions are taken from **the floor** and a vote is taken. If there is an equal number of votes for and against the motion, the chairperson has a final, deciding vote.

Did you know?

This formal way of debating is followed in the House of Commons in London. The House of Commons is the democratically elected house of the UK Parliament, responsible for making laws and checking the work of the Government. Once a year, the UK Youth Parliament (a group of elected teenagers from all over the UK) also meets there to discuss important issues affecting teenagers, ensuring that the opinions and wishes of young people are heard by the nation's policy-makers and politicians.

Key terms

chairperson a person who is in charge of a meeting

motion a statement, idea or policy that is discussed in a debate

opposition a statement that opposes a judgement or opinion

proposition a statement that expresses a judgement or opinion

the floor the formal term to describe everyone participating in a debate apart from the chairperson and main speakers

This house believes… a formal way of introducing a motion

At the end of this unit, you are going to hold a debate on a topic of your choice. The following activities will help you to deepen your knowledge and rehearse the skills that will be needed.

Exploring ideas for and against

When you hold your own debate, you must decide who will speak in favour of the motion and who will speak to oppose it. However, you always need arguments that might be used by either side. This is so that you can anticipate what your opponents might say and have **counter-arguments** ready to address the points they make. Look at an example of a motion for debate below.

> **The motion:** This house believes that being a celebrity is too easy to achieve and too hard to handle.

Firstly, you need to think of arguments in favour of the motion.

> **Arguments FOR the motion**
> - Many celebrities have found constant attention from the media stressful and upsetting.
> - It is possible to become a celebrity simply by being good at using social media.
> - It is possible to become a celebrity without having any special talent or skill just by appearing on a reality TV programme.

For every argument in favour of the motion, you need to think of a counter-argument and other arguments against the motion.

> **Arguments AGAINST the motion**
> - Most celebrities are comfortable with the pressures of being famous because they receive specialist advice on how to handle it.
> - Millions of people use social media but very few have become celebrities.
> - Although some of those who appear on reality TV shows become stars, the vast majority do not.

Activity 2

Add one argument for the motion and one argument against the motion to the lists above.

> 🔑 **Key term**
>
> **counter-argument** an argument that opposes the point put forward

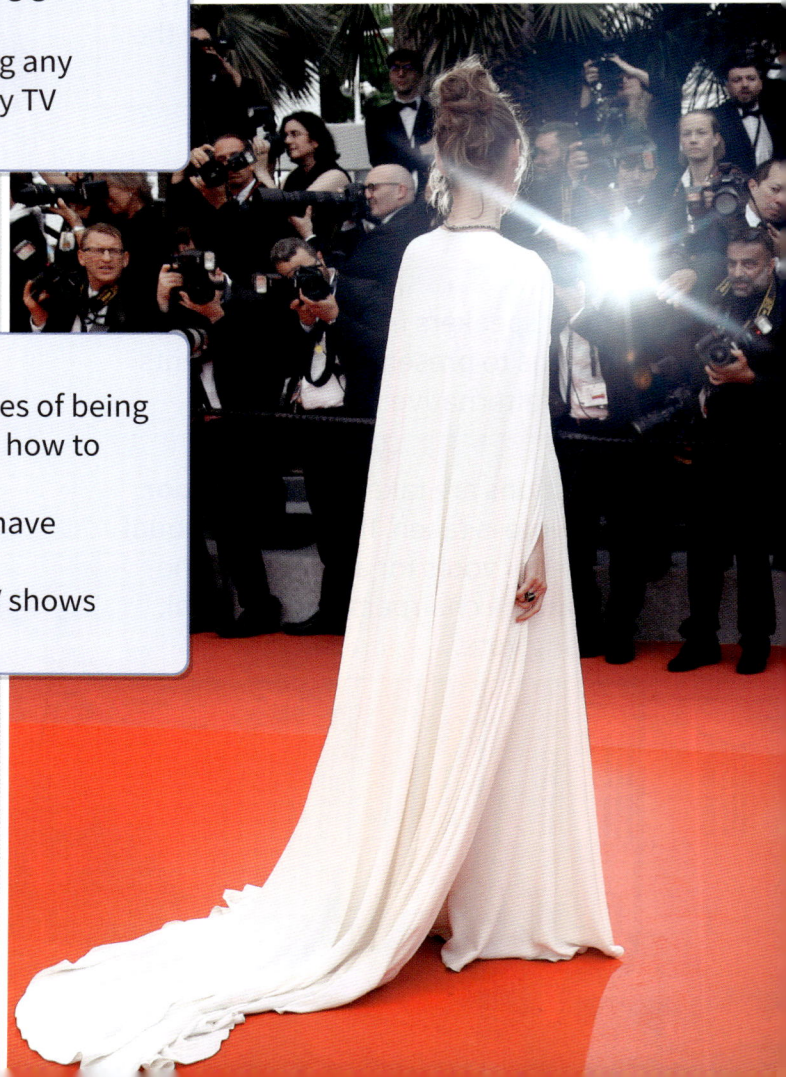

Ordering your ideas

When you have thought of your ideas, you need to select the best ones and put them into a logical sequence by numbering them. It is important to do this so that your ideas flow and your strongest argument is included in the right place for the most impact. For example:

Arguments FOR the motion

1 It is possible to become a celebrity simply by being good at using social media.
2 It is possible to become a celebrity without having any special talent or skill just by appearing on a reality TV programme.
3 Many celebrities have found constant attention from the media stressful and upsetting.

This links directly to the motion, so is placed first.

This builds on the first statement, so is placed second.

This picks up on the second idea in the motion (that being a celebrity is hard to handle) so is included later.

Activity 3

Now look at the statements made *against* the motion opposite and try to put them into a logical order. Explain your reasoning in the way suggested above.

Developing your ideas

The next step is to develop your points further by applying 'the ABC routine'. Think about how you might **A**dd to them; **B**uild on them; or **C**ontest them.

For example, look closely at this argument for the motion on page 26:

> It is possible to become a celebrity without having any special talent or skill just by appearing on a reality TV programme.

You could *add* to this with an appropriate fact, such as:

Indeed, 65 per cent of the stories printed in tabloid newspapers are about contestants on reality TV shows.

Or the statement might be *built* on by developing the thought with:

This undermines the meaning of 'celebrity': it used to be that only people who were extraordinary in some way became famous.

Alternatively, if you don't agree, the statement could be *contested* with a counter-argument:

There are now so many reality TV programmes, and so many people appear on them, that relatively few of those who take part become famous.

Activity 4

Choose another of the statements or counter-arguments opposite and apply 'the ABC routine'.

Building your argument

How you connect your ideas together is important. A logically ordered argument is more persuasive than a set of random points with no apparent links between them.

Discourse markers can help to make connections between points. Read through the different types of discourse markers below and their purposes. These could be included to:

- indicate an additional point, for example 'additionally', 'moreover', 'furthermore'
- highlight the sequence of ideas, for example 'firstly', 'next', 'then'
- introduce a counter-argument, for example 'on the other hand', 'however', 'by contrast'
- show a particular effect, for example 'consequently', 'as a result of this'
- bring everything together, for example 'to conclude', 'in summary'.

> ### 🔑 Key term
>
> **discourse marker** a word or phrase that makes a link between points and organises text

Activity 5

Look back at your arguments explored so far in this unit and choose appropriate discourse markers to connect the statements. One has been done already for you below.

> It is possible to become a celebrity without having any special talent or skill just by appearing on a reality TV programme. *However,* there are now so many reality TV programmes, and so many people appear on them, that relatively few of those who take part become famous.

> ### ⬆ Stretch yourself
>
> List more discourse markers that you think could be used effectively in a debate.

The speeches made by the speakers for the proposition and the speakers for the opposition introduce the main arguments for both sides. They need to be as persuasive as possible.

Activity 6

Look back at Units 1 and 2 to remind yourself of the rhetorical devices and structural choices that are known to influence an audience. Create a checklist of all the language devices that were covered and use it when you come to write your speech.

> ✅ **Tip**
>
> Your list might start like this: rhetorical questions, facts and statistics, emotive language…

🧩 Putting it all together

Activity 7

a Now it is your turn to put all you have learned about debating into practice. As a class, choose a motion from those listed below or invent one of your own. Work through the five steps listed on page 25 to hold the debate.

> This house believes that…
> - teachers should be replaced by robots
> - young people should be paid for doing chores at home
> - exams should be abolished.

b During the debate, listen very carefully to what is said, so that you can respond effectively.

- If you are the speaker or support the speaker, you should aim to highlight, develop and add to the main points.
- If you oppose the speaker, you need to counter the main points made.

c When you have finished your debate, fill in the third column of your KFL grid (see page 24) to record what you have learned. For example, what made some arguments particularly effective? Who was the most persuasive speaker and why? What did you personally find the most difficult thing to do? Think about how you could overcome this next time.

d Look back to your confidence ratings in Activity 1 on page 24. Mark each out of 10 again after you have completed this unit and see if they have improved. Why did your confidence increase or decrease? How did you help yourself?

1.4 How do dramatists convey power?

In this unit, you will:

- learn how dramatists present power through dialogue
- explore how vocabulary and sentence structure can reveal power and status
- write a dramatic scene, showing shifts of power between characters.

What's the big idea?

Previously, you looked at how people can exert power and influence through speeches and debates. You have learned how rhetorical and structural techniques can be used by speakers to persuade others to share their views and to stir them into action.

In this unit, you will look at how dramatists use dialogue to show how power and influence can shift between people. Although drama is fictional, the same shifts in power and influence can be seen in real-life conversations and situations.

Activity 1

a What makes people appear powerful? Look back at the speeches by President Obama and Greta Thunberg in Units 1 and 2.

b What stories can you think of that involve a struggle for power? Remember that power can take many forms, such as personal power in a relationship, political power or military power.

c Look at the list of groups below. Which groups do you think have more power in society? Give reasons for your answers.

i	men or women	iv	teachers or students
ii	adults or children	v	the financially stable or those of limited financial means
iii	politicians or the general public		

✓ Tip

Think about who makes the rules for others to follow. Who decides what activities to do and who does them? Who determines which actions should be rewarded and which should be punished?

The extract opposite is taken from the play *Noughts & Crosses*, which is based on a novel by Malorie Blackman. The play is set in a country torn apart by racial prejudice and conflict between two groups: the Crosses, who are the wealthier and more powerful members of society; and the noughts, who are less powerful and less advantaged.

At this point in the play, Sephy, who is a Cross, has been kidnapped by a gang of noughts. They intend to keep her prisoner until her father pays a ransom for her release. Sephy used to be best friends with Callum, one of the gang now holding her captive.

Extract from *Noughts & Crosses* by Malorie Blackman, dramatised by Dominic Cooke

*Sephy's cell. Callum holds scissors and a **camcorder**.*
He removes Sephy's hood. He goes to cut a lock of
her hair. Their eyes meet.
Jude and Leila stand behind Callum.

5   **Callum**   I want you to hold this newspaper.

    Sephy   Why?

    Jude   I need to film you holding today's paper.

Sephy notices Jude for the first time.

    Sephy   Jude! Might have known you were

10   behind this.

    Callum   It wasn't just him.

    Sephy   Whatever. I'm not going to help you.

Callum goes to cut her hair again. Jude holds her
down.

15   **Jude**   Hold that paper or we'll break your
       arms.

    Callum   *[To Jude]* I don't need you standing over
       me, supervising.

    Jude   Not supervising. Just observing.

20   **Callum**   Hold the newspaper, Sephy.

Callum holds the paper out. Sephy takes it. Leila, a
fellow nought kidnapper, enters.

    Leila   I've come to see the daughter of the
       famous Kamal Hadley.

25   **Callum**   I don't need an audience, thanks.

    Leila   Let's see the silver spoon then.

    Callum   Leila!

    Leila   I bet you've never had more to worry
       about in your life than chipping the
30   odd fingernail.

    Jude   Leila, go and guard the front. Morgan,
       you go with her. [...]

Callum hands Sephy a sheet of paper.

    Callum   I want you to read out that message
35   for your father.

Callum points the camcorder at her. She scrunches
the paper up and throws it away.

    Sephy   *[To the camera]* Dad, don't give them a
       penny.

40 *Jude rushes over to her and grabs her.*

    Jude   You're not in control in here. We are.
       And you will do as you're told or you
       won't leave this place alive. Do you
       understand? [...]

45   **Callum**   I'll handle this.

Jude goes to exit. He turns back.

    Jude   Make sure she does as she's told.

Jude goes out. Callum picks up the paper and starts
smoothing it.

50   **Sephy**   I understand why you feel you have to
       do something. I really do. But this isn't
       the way.

Pause.

       Callum, listen to me. At **Chivers** I
55   became involved in protests and
       debates and **sit-ins**. If you try to
       change the world using violence, you'll
       just swap one form of injustice for –

    Callum   I don't want your ruddy advice thank
60   you. I'm sick of your charity and your
       handouts. You're just like all the others.
       You think we noughts can't do a
       damned thing unless you Crosses are
       there to help or supervise.

65   **Sephy**   Don't hate me for wanting to make a
       difference. I genuinely –

    Callum   Shut up! Hold up the newspaper and
       read the words on this.

---

camcorder – a camera that records videos

Chivers – a boarding school where Sephy is sent

sit-ins – a type of protest where protestors sit down and refuse to move

⭐ Boosting your vocabulary

Skilled writers choose their words with care. The activity below focuses on some key vocabulary in the source text, which has been highlighted on page 31.

Activity 2

Callum tells Jude he doesn't want him 'supervising' his treatment of Sephy. He also accuses Sephy of being like all other Crosses, assuming they need to 'supervise' everything. Both these words use the prefix 'super-' meaning 'over' or 'greater', and also part of the Latin word *visum*, meaning 'vision' or 'that which is seen'.

a   Use this information to explain the meaning of the verb 'to supervise'.

b   Why do you think the playwright chose to use the word 'supervise' here, rather than 'watch', for example? Think about what it suggests about who has the most power.

c   How does this reflect what Callum feels about his level of power and authority in relation to the other characters in the play?

d   Jude describes what he is doing as 'observing'. How does this differ from 'supervising'?

e   Do you agree that Jude is just 'observing'? Explain your opinion with reference to other things that Jude says or does in the playscript.

f   Here are some **synonyms** for the word 'observe'. Rank them in order of intensity. Explain the reasons for your order.

look at   watch   contemplate   study

survey   scrutinise   view

✏️ g   Write two sentences. Use the word 'observe' in one sentence and 'supervise' in the other.

✅ Tip

Think about the different **connotations** of each word. Some words might be more suitable in some contexts than others.

🔑 Key terms

connotation an idea or feeling linked to a word, as well as its main meaning

synonym a word or phrase that means the same, or almost the same, as another word or phrase

Building your knowledge

When you read through the extract, you will notice how power shifts between the characters. The author is making structural choices about who is in control and when to impact the audience at different points in the extract. For example, sometimes certain characters give orders and others follow them. At other times, the situation is reversed – this is purposefully done to change how we feel towards the characters at different points in the text. In the next activity, you will need to **infer** how the structural choices and 'shifts' the author has used impact the audience.

Key term

infer to work something out from what is seen, said or done, even though it is not stated directly

Activity 3

a Write the names of the four characters on separate sticky notes. Then read lines 1–4 in the extract (the opening stage directions).

  i Who do you think is the most powerful at this point? Arrange the four sticky notes in order, putting who you think is the most powerful at the top and who is the least powerful at the bottom. You might need to infer who is the most powerful by looking at the types of words they use.

  ii Write a line of dialogue that each character might say to explain the reasons for this order. For example:

> Sephy might say, "I am the least powerful character because I am the prisoner of the others." Alternatively, she might argue that "I am the most powerful character because I am a Cross and the others are noughts."

b Now read lines 5–12.

  i Who appears to be the most powerful now? Re-arrange the sticky notes to reflect any changes in the rank order of power.

  ii Write a line of dialogue for each character to explain any changes in the rank order.

c Read lines 13–45 and look carefully at what Callum and Jude say to each other and to the other characters. Note also how they behave towards each other and how other characters respond to them.

  i What do the characters' words suggest about who is the most powerful in the scene? Similarly, what do the characters' actions and reactions reveal about who has the most control over the others?

  ii Adjust your order of sticky notes to reflect who holds the most power when Jude leaves the cell. As before, write a line of dialogue for each character to explain this order.

Dramatists convey a character's power not just by *what* they say, but also *how* they say it. For example:

- Jude uses commands or **imperatives**, such as "Leila, go and guard the front", which reflects his desire to take control.
- Sephy uses **declarative** sentences to make a forceful statement. Her declaration "I'm not going to help you," shows that she is powerful, determined and refuses to back down, even when she feels intimidated.
- Interruptions can be a display of power, as they cut off someone's flow of speech and stop them from expressing themselves. Another language feature that can display power is **sarcasm** because it can belittle and mock someone.

> ## 🔑 Key terms
>
> **declarative** a sentence that makes a statement
>
> **imperative** a sentence that gives an order, command or instruction
>
> **interrogative** a sentence that asks a question
>
> **sarcasm** the use of humour or saying the opposite of what is meant to mock or criticise someone

Activity 4

a Answer the questions below, noting what this suggests about the power held by the characters.

The first one has been done for you.

Question	Answer	What this suggests about the power held by the character and why
Who has the most lines?	Callum	This suggests that Callum is the most powerful in the scene because the audience's attention is most often on him.
Who speaks the most words?		
Who uses the most imperatives?		
Who uses the most declaratives?		
Who uses the most **interrogatives**?		
Who uses sarcasm?		

✏ b i Write three more sentences to add to the dialogue in the extract. They can fit at any point and be spoken by any character(s). Make one sentence an imperative, another a declarative and another an interrogative.

ii Explain what your lines show about the character's feelings and sense of power or control.

BLACK AND WHITE.
RIGHT AND WRONG.

INCLUDES THE
SHORT STORY,
CALLUM

NOUGHTS & CROSSES

malorie blackman

Children's Laureate 2013-2015

Putting it all together

Dramatists use characters' actions and words to show both who has power and who wants power. They shape dialogue to reflect how power can shift between characters in the course of a scene, using declaratives, interrogatives and imperatives to do this.

Activity 5

It's your turn to write a scene using the techniques you have learned about, showing how power can shift between characters.

Follow the steps below.

Step 1: Decide on two or three characters and give them names.

Step 2: Think of a situation in which the characters all want different outcomes, for example:
- friends at the cinema but keen to see different films
- a young person trying to convince an adult to buy a particular item of clothing
- a group lost on a walk and deciding the best thing to do about it.

Step 3: Think about how the characters could try to influence the others in a discussion.
- What might they say and how might they say it?
- How might characters use irony and sarcasm to get their way?
- What sentence types will be most effective?
Choose your vocabulary carefully. Remember that some words and expressions convey authority and power more than others.

Step 4: When you have written your scene, rehearse it in a small group. Listen carefully to how the actors read it, then make edits to the text to make it more dramatic or convincing.

> ✓ **Tip**
>
> For Activity 5, think about the personalities of your characters. It may not be the character that says the most who ultimately has most power.

1.5 How is humour used in poetry?

In this unit, you will:

- learn how humour can influence readers' responses
- explore how sound patterns and structures convey the message of a poem
- write your own poem using a modelled structure.

What's the big idea?

There is a famous saying: 'The pen is mightier than the sword.' It means that writing is more powerful than violence and that words can have a greater influence on people's thoughts and actions than acts of aggression.

In the first part of this chapter, you looked at how people use words to influence others through powerful speeches and debates. You have also looked at how power and influence are conveyed through dialogue in drama and in everyday life. In this unit, you will look at how a poem can convey a powerful message, through humour and skilful use of words and form.

Activity 1

a Do you agree that words can be more powerful than weapons? Which do you think has more impact on the way people think and act?

b Discuss any speeches, novels, plays, poems or films that have had a powerful effect on people or that have influenced your own thinking and actions.

c How can humour be used to influence an audience? Think about comedy in all forms, such as novels, plays, films, television and stand-up comedy. Can humour help to convey a serious message?

Key terms

quatrain a stanza of four lines, often with a strict rhythm and rhyme scheme

rhyme using the same sound to end words, particularly at the ends of lines

rhythm the pattern of beats in a line of music or poetry

Brian Bilston's poem 'Make Poetry Not War' uses humour to urge world leaders who wage wars to spend more time writing poetry instead. It is linked to the idea that the 'pen' is a better choice of weapon than the 'sword'.

The poem is written as a series of **quatrains** (four-line stanzas that usually **rhyme**). The **rhythm** this creates is also used to reinforce the message.

'Make Poetry Not War' by Brian Bilston

Leaders of the world,
stop your fighting.
Invest your time
in poetry writing.

5 Enough of all those
military manoeuvres,
concentrate on
more **literary oeuvres**.

Think about the planet,
10 when you plan
to drop a bomb upon it,
pause, ponder, then pen a **sonnet**.

Or if there's somebody
who doesn't like u,
15 appease them with
a humble **haiku.**

Let words be your weapons,
Metaphors your missiles.
Search out strident stanzas.
20 Ditch your **Trident planzas.**

Write a peace poem about a pipe
an olive branch, a dove.
Take a ticket to Tender Town,
aboard the quatrain of love.

military manoeuvres – exercises carried out by the armed forces in preparation for warfare
literary oeuvres – works of literature
sonnet – a poem of 14 lines with rhymes
haiku – a Japanese poetic form that consists of three lines with five syllables in the first, seven in the second and five in the last
Trident – a nuclear missile system
planzas – a made-up word to say 'plans' and rhyme with 'stanzas'

⭐ Boosting your vocabulary

Skilled writers choose their words with care. The activity below focuses on some key vocabulary in the source text, which has been highlighted on page 37.

Activity 2

a   The word 'invest' has many meanings. Which meaning below is relevant in the context of this poem?

| to use money to make a profit | to spend time or effort on something useful or worthwhile | to give a title or power to someone |

b   Why do you think the poet uses the word 'invest' rather than 'spend'?

c   The word 'appease' means to make someone feel calm or quiet by giving them what they want. It is linked to the French words *à paix* meaning 'to peace'. How does this information help you to understand the meaning of the word 'appease'?

d   The fifth stanza encourages the reader to be more aggressive with their language. How does the word 'strident' add to this effect? Think about the meaning of the word and how it is used in the poem.

💡 Building your knowledge

Bilston's poem addresses the serious topic of warfare in a light-hearted, humorous way. He uses language playfully to amuse his readers. This makes war and those who wage it seem less frightening and less powerful.

Bilston plays with the *sounds* of words, to create patterns and unexpected relationships to amuse the reader. He also uses repetition of sentence style to help structure the poem, and very short lines to give impact to his message.

When analysing poetry, you should look at how the writer has used the following poetic devices:

- sound patterns
- language features
- structure, including line length
- rhyme schemes.

> ✅ **Tip**
>
> Remember these poetic devices and use them to analyse any poem.

Activity 3

Below is a list of language features that relate to the sounds of words.

rhyme: words that end with the same sound, e.g. doors/floors

assonance: words that contain the same middle vowel sounds, e.g. toast/loaf

alliteration: words that begin with the same sound, e.g. flying footballs

consonance: words that contain the same consonant sounds, e.g. fake/wicket

a   Which of these features have you heard of before?

b   Match the features above to the quotations below from Bilston's poem.

drop/bomb   fighting/writing   pause/ponder/pen   take/ticket

c   Add more of your own examples to at least three of the definitions. They do not need to be in the poem.

Bilston uses a series of imperatives (commands) to structure the poem. These tell leaders what he thinks they should be doing instead of fighting a war. For example, he tells them to 'stop your fighting' and 'Think about the planet'. The imperative form is powerful and assertive.

Activity 4

a   List the other imperatives in the poem.

b   What tone does this create? Imagine how you might read these lines aloud. This might help you to describe a suitable tone.

c   Write two more lines for the poem that start with an imperative.

> ✅ **Tip**
>
> In Activity 4, remember that you are giving an instruction to the leaders of the world about what else they should be doing, preferably linked to creative writing. The lines do not need to rhyme.

Activity 5

The lines of the poem are very short, making the writer's points succinct.

a   Do you think the reader can appreciate word choices more in shorter lines than in longer lines?

b   Do short lines quicken or slow the pace of the poem?

c   Do you think short lines are more or less powerful than longer lines?

Bilston's poem is written in a series of quatrains. The poet makes humorous reference to the form in the last two lines: 'Take a ticket to Tender Town, / aboard the *quatrain* of love.'

The four lines of quatrains often follow strict rhythm and rhyme schemes. We describe rhyming patterns by using letters to identify the lines that rhyme. The sound at the end of the first line is given the letter A. So, the rhyme pattern in the first stanza is ABCB.

Bilston's poem includes a **rhyming couplet** in the fifth stanza: 'Search out strident stanzas. / Ditch your Trident planzas.' In a rhyming couplet, the words at the end of the two lines rhyme, so the rhyme scheme is AA.

Leaders of the world,	A
stop your fighting.	B
Invest your time	C
in poetry writing.	B

Activity 6

a What two rhyme patterns does Bilston use?

b Using rhyme often causes the reader to notice particular pairs of words. Look at the pairs of rhyming words that Bilston uses in his poem. Discuss the following questions with a partner.

   i Do any of the pairs surprise or amuse you?

   ii Do any shock you or make you pause to think more deeply about their meaning?

   iii Which words gain emphasis from being part of a rhyming pair? Why might these words seem significant?

c Think of some rhyming words that could be used in a rhyming couplet on the same theme as Bilston's poem. There are some examples below.

> grenade/parade   wrong/song   worse/verse

d Choose one pair of your own and write a rhyming couplet including those words. An example has been included below to help you.

> Resist that deadly hand grenade
>
> Turn to celebrations and parade

❓ Did you know?

Quatrains are one of the oldest poetic forms and appear in the poetry of many different countries and cultures. Quatrains from ancient Persian poetry use four lines that all rhyme. Quatrains known as 'the heroic stanza' have alternate lines rhyming.

🔑 Key term

rhyming couplet two consecutive lines of poetry that have rhyming final words

Putting it all together

Activity 7

Now it is your turn to write a quatrain. Try to use humour to make your message more powerful and influence the reader to share your way of thinking.

Step 1: Choose a topic and write down some key words connected to your topic. For example, below are words that might go into a poem about the high wages of Premier League footballers.

> football   wages   goal   millionaire   match

Step 2: Think of words that rhyme with the ones you have chosen. Here are some suggestions.

> **football** – recall, appal, enthral, install, netball

> **wages** – ages, enrages, cages, stages, pages

> **millionaire** – anywhere, armchair, declare, despair

Step 3: Use the words to create a rhyming couplet.

> Here's a topic that always enrages:
> The size of footballers' weekly wages
> Something that drives me to despair:
> A football player millionaire

Step 4: Now combine any two of the couplets or build on one to make it into a quatrain.

Step 5: Build your poem by adding quatrains. Use some of the techniques explored earlier to amuse and entertain your reader, such as surprising use of vocabulary and playing with word sounds.

Stretch yourself

Swap your work with a partner and analyse the effects of the techniques they have used to entertain the reader.

1.6 What is the power of the press?

In this unit, you will:

- learn about the form and purpose of editorials
- explore techniques writers use to engage and persuade the reader
- comment on the effectiveness of a newspaper editorial.

What's the big idea?

The media can communicate with very large audiences, making it an extremely powerful tool for anyone wanting to influence public opinion. For example, in newspaper editorials, the journalist could write about a topic they feel strongly about, hoping to influence people's thinking and actions.

In the last unit, you looked at how poetry and humour can be used to convey powerful ideas to an audience. In this unit, you will consider the power and influence of the media as a whole, and editorials in particular, on people's attitudes and behaviour.

⚙ Activity 1

a Read the statements below about **the media**. Decide whether you agree or disagree with them.

> Television charity appeals raise money for good causes.

> Newspapers purposefully include rhetorical devices to persuade and influence their readers.

> Violent films encourage violent behaviour.

> Television talent competitions allow ordinary people to become stars.

> Newspapers select what to report and decide how to report it.

> People are influenced by advertising to buy certain food and drinks.

b There is a saying, 'With great power comes great responsibility.' Do you think the media behaves responsibly? Is it responsible if the media uses rhetorical devices that are persuasive in a subtle way? Share your ideas and explain your answer in a discussion.

🔑 Key terms

editorial a newspaper article expressing a writer's opinion

the media all means of communicating with a large audience through various outlets, such as television broadcasting, advertising, newspapers and the Internet

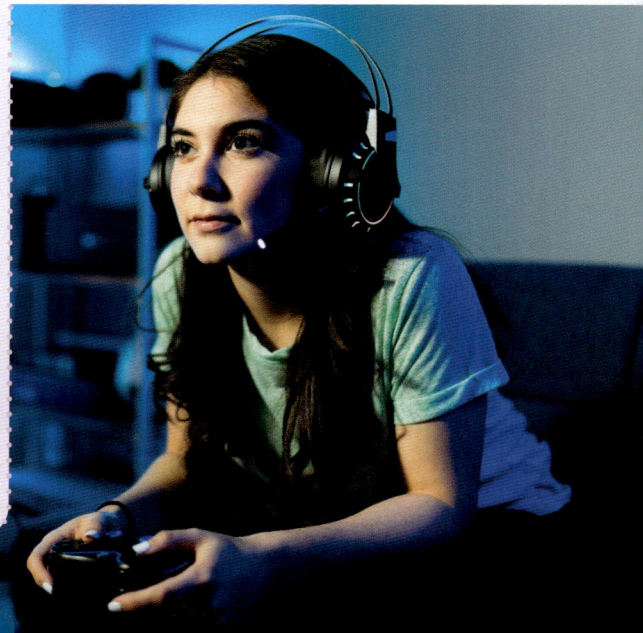

The extract below is from a newspaper **editorial** from *The Guardian*. It focuses on the benefits of video games. Gaming is a popular hobby but can sometimes be controversial.

Activity 2

With a partner, talk about your opinion of video games. What do you like about them? What do you dislike about them? Do other people in your life have different feelings about gaming?

Video games can improve mental health. Let's stop seeing them as a guilty pleasure

by Keza MacDonald

After an Oxford study this week showed that people who play more video games report greater well-being, the headlines reflected a sense of stunned **incredulity**. "Playing video games
5 BENEFITS mental health," exclaimed MailOnline, while Business Insider went with "Video games might actually be good for you." […]

But why the surprise? For anyone who actually plays video games, this is hardly news. Video
10 games are fun and interesting, and doing fun, interesting things makes you happy. Would we need a study to show that watching a few episodes of a beloved TV show makes you feel good, or that sitting down with a good book is
15 relaxing? This year especially, video games have been an essential form of escapism and therapy for millions, and this study proves that I was hardly the only one devotedly playing Animal Crossing to **decompress** after an intense day. [...]

20 If you look at the way video games are still **predominantly** covered on TV and in the news, however, it's easy to see why a study about their positive effects might prompt such shock. It speaks to a bafflingly **persistent** negative **stigma**:
25 video games are still seen by many as, at best, a waste of time, and at worst downright sinister. Coverage always focuses on how much money the video games industry makes, and how violent they may or may not be. Every time a game gets
30 popular with kids, the columns and TV news segments take on a **wary**, **alarmist** tone […].

I've been on the sharp end of this baffling stigma since 2005, when I first started writing professionally about video games as a teenager.

35 According to market research firm Newzoo, there are nearly 3 billion gamers in the world. What the vast majority of them get out of their hobby is positive and life-enhancing. I cannot tell you how many people I've met who've
40 credited games for helping them manage their depression, stress or anxiety, or just the everyday difficulties of life. […]

Will people ever finally stop characterising video games as either a guilty pleasure or an
45 insidious force, and instead acknowledge that they are no different from film or music or TV? That there are good games and bad games, serious games and entertaining games, and that they make people happy? There are so
50 many more interesting conversations to be had than "are video games somehow bad for you?" and "gosh, look how much money this industry makes". Try talking to people who actually play them, which these days is 85% of people under
55 35 and plenty of older folks too, and you'll find the real stories.

---

incredulity – disbelief

decompress – relax

predominantly – mostly

persistent – continuing; refusing to stop

stigma – negative or unfair beliefs about something

wary – careful, uncertain

alarmist – creating unnecessary fear or panic

⭐ Boosting your vocabulary

Skilled writers choose their words with care. The activity below focuses on some key vocabulary in the source text, which has been highlighted on page 43.

highlighted on page 43.

> 🗝 **Key term**
>
> **antonym** a word that has the opposite meaning of a particular word

Activity 3

a The writer refers to how gaming can be a form of 'escapism' for some people.

  i What do you think this word means?

  ii What other activities do you think might offer people a form of 'escapism'?

b 'Sinister' is a synonym for 'evil'.

  i Why do you think the writer chose such a strong adjective to describe how some people view video games? What does it suggest about what she thinks of those views?

  ii Write a sentence of your own, using the word 'sinister'.

c The writer suggests that some people view video games as an 'insidious force'. What does she mean by this? Complete the Frayer model below to explore the word 'insidious'. Refer to a completed Frayer model on page 56 if you need to.

Frayer model

Definition	Characteristics

Word
insidious

Examples	Antonyms

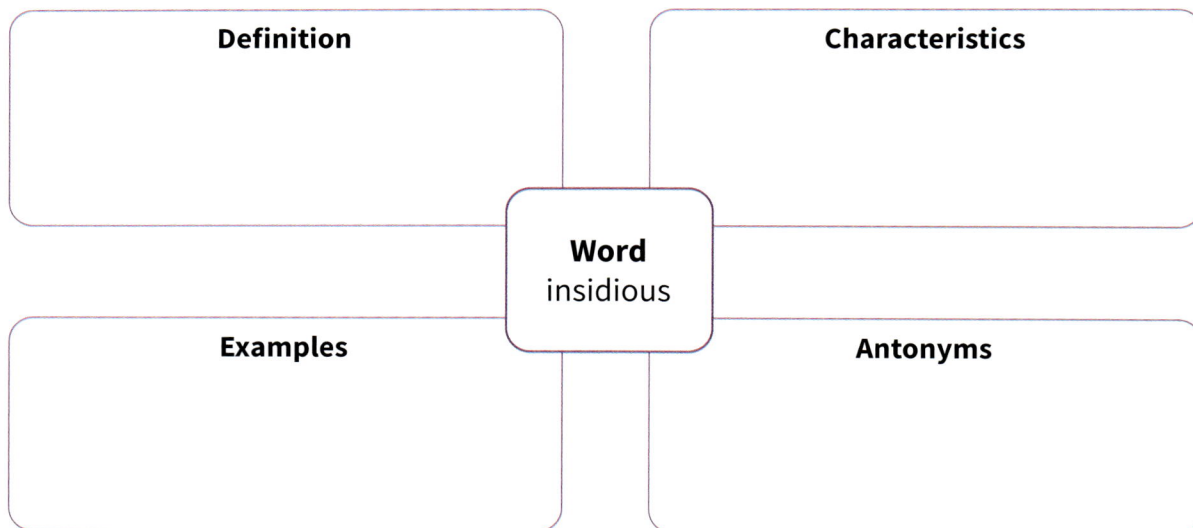

d The writer uses all the words above in relation to different views about gaming. What sort of impression do they help to build of the different opinions about the impact of video games? Give reasons for your answer.

Building your knowledge

Editorials are articles that are written to express a journalist's opinion.
There are four types of editorials:

news-focused editorials: these comment on an issue that is currently in the news	**critical editorials:** these explore a problem, identify possible causes and suggest solutions
celebratory editorials: these celebrate a particular person, profession or organisation	**persuasive editorials:** these aim to persuade the reader to take a particular position on a topic

Activity 4

a What type of editorial is 'Video games can improve mental health. Let's stop seeing them as a guilty pleasure'?

b How do you know what type of editorial it is?

An effective editorial captures a reader's attention from the start and holds it to the very last sentence so that it conveys its message and meets its purpose.

Editorials often influence readers by mixing personal opinions with statements of fact. In this way, a writer's personal opinions can sound as if they have more authority. For example, in the editorial on page 43, the writer states that gaming can be good for people's well-being. She references an Oxford study to support this statement.

However, in other places the writer asserts an opinion with no evidence to back it up. For example, she says that 'video games are still seen by many as, at best, a waste of time, and at worst downright sinister'. This is just the writer's opinion: it is stated as a fact but no evidence is given.

Activity 5

Read the editorial on page 43 again.

a Identify the statements that have been supported by facts and statistics.

b Identify the emotive language that has been used.

c Which is the most persuasive to a reader?

The writer of the editorial uses a variety of literary techniques and rhetorical devices to hold the reader's interest and to influence their viewpoint.

Activity 6

a Match up the techniques listed below with the effects they have on the reader. The first one has been done for you. Then find examples of these techniques in the editorial on page 43.

Techniques

- rhetorical questions
- first person plural pronouns 'we', 'us', 'ours'
- second person pronoun 'you'
- emotive language
- parallelism
- anecdotes (examples from everyday life)
- humour
- different viewpoints

Effects

- lightens a serious tone
- the similar grammatical structure creates emphasis
- provokes a strong emotional response
- questions that engage the reader and make them think
- suggest that the writer and audience share the same views
- varies perspectives
- provides examples that readers can identify with
- creates a sense of relationship by addressing the reader directly

b Develop your answer into a short piece of analytical writing. Structure your response by first identifying the technique, then giving an example (from the text), and then developing the point further. For example:

> The writer engages the readers by using rhetorical questions. For example, — Technique
> 'Would we need a study to show that watching a few episodes of a beloved TV — Example
> show makes you feel good, or that sitting down with a good book is relaxing?'
> These not only make the readers think, but also help to persuade the reader — Development
> to share the writer's viewpoint.

Activity 7

Editorials are written to influence public opinion. Has this editorial changed your views on video games? Explain why or why not.

> ✔ **Tip**
>
> All of the techniques listed in Activity 6 have been covered in previous units. Look back for a reminder of them.

Putting it all together

In this unit you have learned about the purpose of editorials and how writers use language, structure and form to fulfil that purpose. Read the extract from an editorial below. It was written in response to a wealthy Dartmoor landowner, Alexander Darwall, winning a court case that allowed landowners the right to refuse wild camping (camping in the natural landscape).

Activity 8

✏ Using the knowledge and skills you have gained in this unit, comment on how effective you think the editorial below is in engaging and influencing readers. Consider the following in your answer:

- the type of editorial it is
- the headline
- the use of facts and opinions
- the use of rhetorical devices, such as rhetorical questions and emotive language.

> ✅ **Tip**
>
> Look back at the work you did in Unit 2. What skills do you notice you used in that unit that you are also using here? How can you use this work to help you?

The Dartmoor wild camping ban further limits our right to roam. It must be fought.

by Sophie Pavelle

When I did the **Ten Tors** challenge at school in 2013, I would fight back tears with my teammates, anticipating the relief and joy we would feel at crossing the finish line after
5 45 miles of backpacking on Dartmoor. On Friday, different tears fell. Messages flooded my phone announcing that the right to wild camp on Dartmoor had been overturned in an astonishing defeat. [...]

10 Until Friday, an assumed right to wild camp under a bylaw in the Dartmoor Commons Act 1985 saw thousands of people enjoying this most basic, fundamental form of human recreation – without having to seek landowners'
15 permission. [...]

For Darwall, Dartmoor's sixth-largest landowner, the right to wild camp in England's largest national park never existed. For someone like me, who has spent a young
20 lifetime walking Dartmoor's landscape, what does that mean? The friendships formed in howling winds and under red skies, the boy I met and will marry, the questions I've yelled, the answers I've found, the shelters from the
25 storm – were they all in my head?

This loss leaves the kind of grief that only nature can muster – and sustain. This grief is fuelling a wildfire of outrage in all who have been touched by the moors. [...]

30 People are right to be angry. Britain's wildlife, and the right to enjoy it, are under attack. Britain has lost more biodiversity than any other **G7** nation, and ranks bottom in Europe for nature connectedness. The Right To Roam
35 campaign, which advocates for better access to nature in England, reminds us that we are banned from 92% of English land.

Ten Tors challenge – a camping challenge for teenagers run by the British army

G7 – the international Group of Seven, a political forum consisting of seven countries

1.7 How do adverts persuade people?

In this unit, you will:

- learn how visual advertisements attract attention and influence people

- explore how symbols, slogans and rhetorical devices can convey powerful messages simply

- write an advertisement to influence people's behaviour.

What's the big idea?

The purpose of most advertisements (adverts) is to persuade people to buy a product or to deliver a message quickly, simply and with impact.

In the last two units you explored how poetry and newspaper editorials can be written to influence people's ideas and actions. In this unit, you will look at how adverts, including public messages, can catch people's attention and convey important, powerful messages in a simple, memorable way.

⚙ Activity 1

a List any adverts that you remember seeing in the last week. Where did you see them? For example, it could be on buildings, transport or on your phone.

b What advertising do you see at school? Think about:
  - branding that you might see on clothes, shoes, food items and posters
  - logos, mottoes and slogans linked to your school
  - motivational posters
  - adverts for school clubs, societies, sporting events and theatrical performances.

c Of all the advertising that you have seen, which most affects the way you think and the way you behave?

Most of the adverts we see today are part of bigger, complex marketing campaigns. It is usually the combination of the different parts of the campaign that influences people's opinions and actions. Most adverts nowadays are **multimodal**, which means that they combine words with visual images to make meaning.

Activity 2

Look at the two posters below. They were both part of big Government public health campaigns.

a   Identify the purpose, audience and format of these texts.

b   One of these posters was published during the Second World War (1939–1945). The other poster was published in 2020. Which do you think was published when? Give reasons for your answers.

? Did you know?

We think of advertising as a modern invention, but picture adverts for shops and trademarks for products date back to ancient Egypt, Greece and Rome.

🔑 Key term

multimodal having or involving many methods (modes), e.g. text, images, motion, audio

Poster 1

CATCH IT

Germs spread easily. Always carry tissues and use them to catch your cough or sneeze.

BIN IT

Germs can live for several hours on tissues. Dispose of your tissue as soon as possible.

KILL IT

Hands can transfer germs to every surface you touch. Clean your hands as soon as you can.

NHS

Poster 2

MINISTRY OF HEALTH *says:—*

Coughs and sneezes spread diseases

Trap the germs by using your handkerchief

Help to keep the Nation Fighting Fit

⭐ Boosting your vocabulary

Skilled writers choose their words with care. Adverts use very few words, so each word is important and needs to contribute to the overall message.

Activity 3

a Look again at Poster 1 and Poster 2 on page 49. If someone glanced at Poster 2 quickly and just read five key words, which words would get the message across? Explain your answer carefully.

b The word 'advert' is linked to the Latin word *advertere*, which means 'to turn towards'. Explain how these meanings are linked.

c Poster 1 tells people to 'Dispose of your tissue as soon as possible'. Below are some synonyms for 'dispose of'.

deal with   scrap   finish with   destroy

jettison   dump   throw away

Why do you think the writer chose 'dispose of' rather than these alternatives? Think about the tone of the message and the effect that the writer wants to create.

Building your knowledge

Some messages rely on pictures or **symbols** to represent something complex or abstract in a simple, clear way. In mathematics, the symbol '+' represents addition. In music, the notes on a score represent sounds. In stories, the character of a lion can represent courage. Road signs, emojis and cartoons are all symbols and can convey messages visually, powerfully and simply.

> ### ✓ Tip
>
> Remember a connotation is an idea or feeling linked to a word, as well as its main meaning.

Activity 4

a   What messages or ideas do each of the images below convey?

i    ii    iii    iv    v

b   Look at the images on the posters on page 49. What message or ideas do they convey, and why?

Adverts and posters are often multimodal like the examples on page 49. This means they include pictures, as well as words, to reinforce the overall message. Some pictures **summarise** the words in a simple, memorable, visual way while others carry details that have more connotations. Poster 2 shows women making shells (explosive devices) in a wartime ammunitions factory. There are fewer shells in front of the sneezing person and they are untidy, compared with the person next to her. This suggests that by not sticking to government health advice, the worker is not as efficient and effective as the others.

The text of an advertisement often includes rhetorical devices to make the message memorable and persuade the reader. These devices turn a message into a powerful, memorable **slogan**. Slogans are usually short and summarise a key idea or message. They are designed to be remembered and repeated by audiences to influence as many people as possible. The **tricolon** of imperatives in 'Catch it. Bin it. Kill it' is far more memorable and influential as a slogan than 'Capture your germs and put them into a wastebin to destroy them'.

> ### 🔑 Key terms
>
> **slogan** a short, catchy word or phrase used to advertise something or represent the aims of a campaign or organisation
>
> **summarise** to give the key points
>
> **symbol** something specific that represents a more general quality or situation
>
> **tricolon** a pattern of three words or phrases grouped together to be memorable and have impact

Look at the poster from the Merseyside Police Department below.
It uses an image and text to convey a powerful message.

Activity 5

a   What is the purpose of the poster?

b   What does the image of the broken Christmas tree decoration suggest?

c   How does the image reinforce the message conveyed by the words?

d   The text on the advertisement uses many rhetorical devices. Find an example of:

   i   an imperative

   ii   parallelism

   iii   a second person pronoun, used to address the audience directly.

e   What is the effect of each of these devices?

> **✓ Tip**
>
> All these rhetorical devices have been covered in previous units. Look back to remind yourself of their definitions and the effects that they create for the reader.

> **↑ Stretch yourself**
>
> Try to convey the message of the advertisement in a tricolon.

Activity 6

Poster 1 and Poster 2 on page 49 use rhetorical devices in similar ways for similar purposes.

a   Look at the rhetorical devices listed below. Find examples of each device in one or both of the posters. For example:

> imperative: 'Clean your hands as soon as you can' (Poster 1)
> 'Trap the germs by using your handkerchief' (Poster 2)

| imperative | rhyme | declarative | tricolon | alliteration | repetition |

b   Explain the effect of each rhetorical device. How does it emphasise the message? For example, alliteration links words to create a memorable phrase.

Activity 7

Use one or more of the rhetorical devices you have identified to create a slogan that will encourage one of the following:

- members of your school to walk on the left-hand side of the corridor
- teenagers to behave responsibly on social media
- young children to avoid playing in dangerous places.

Putting it all together

In this unit, you have learned that the combination of slogans, text, images and symbols can create powerfully persuasive adverts to convey important messages.

Activity 8

Now create an advert of your own that uses a slogan, an image, and a short amount of text to do one of the following:

- persuade people to use less electricity
- encourage young children to grow vegetables
- motivate teenagers to try a new hobby
- urge members of your school to support a charity of their choice.

Remember to use some of the features explored in this unit when creating your advert, such as imperatives, repetition and alliteration.

1.8 How does informal language influence others?

In this unit, you will:

- learn how informal language can influence some audiences
- explore the use of non-standard English, including abbreviations and colloquial expressions
- comment on the language used in an article about teenage influencers.

What's the big idea?

Many people regularly post information about themselves on social media. Some attract many followers and become 'influencers' who can guide the opinions and actions of their followers. Influencers often share personal information with their followers, using informal language like that of friends.

In this unit, you will look at how writers adapt their language to communicate with different audiences, in particular through social media.

⚙ Activity 1

a   Think about who might influence your thinking and the decisions you make. Complete a table like the one below, adding some rows of your own.

Decisions	Family	Friends	Teachers	Celebrities
What to wear				
How to behave towards others				
What to read or watch				
What sports teams to support				
What music to listen to				
Who to follow on social media				

b   Look at your table again. Why do you think these people have influence over these things?

c   Discuss when and where these people influence you (e.g. at home, online, at school). What sort of language do they use? Is it informal and friendly or do they use a more formal tone?

The following text is from a webpage of an agency that works with teenage influencers. Its purpose is to introduce these influencers to businesses interested in working with them, but also to engage other teenagers wanting to become influencers. Note that some texts can have multiple different audiences.

As you read the text, think about how its language and style might appeal to its intended audiences.

> ## ✅ Tip
>
> Remember that the purpose of a text is the reason why it is written. The audience is the group (or groups) of people that the text is aimed at, who the writer is hoping to influence.

Teen Influencers Showing Us How It's Done

by Nicole P. Dunford

You know that they say the early bird gets the worm. In this round-up of teen influencers, you'll **discover** young adults on the path to greatness (yes, it sounds like part of a speech from a movie, but it's true). Some have hundreds of thousands of followers, others are at the beginning of their influencer journey. One thing that links them all – they're tackling the influencer game with confidence and putting in the work at an early age.

Megan

With over 155k followers and an **engagement rate** of 3.6% on her **mom-monitored account**, there's no doubt that her self-expression through fashion has connected with teens and young adults not only in the USA but all over the world.

Need to know where she gets her clothing from? Thankfully, Megan shares all the outfit deets in every post so followers everywhere can rock the looks too! Her captions are almost always positive, uplifting, and **inspiring**, giving us much-needed reminders of how awesome we are: 'You are made of magic.' Yes, I am! […]

Viraj

Viraj, a teen video creator from India, is a self-proclaimed '**memer**' with a fantastic sense of humour and a love for health and skincare.

The only male to make our teen influencers list, Viraj is a master at the collab game. He has several featured partnerships throughout his feed with brands in the health, skincare, fashion, and phone accessories industries to name a few. While he definitely injects his infectious sense of humour with his over 7k Instagram followers, Viraj's message of living a healthy life is first and foremost. […]

From their **unique** personalities to their approach to content delivery, […] it's clear that these teen influencers are on the rise and can only get better from here.

Think You Have What It Takes To Be Featured In Our Article?

Then we want to hear from you! Drop us a DM on any of our socials or hook up with us on here. Or why not just register with us right now!

---

engagement rate – the percentage of followers who have interacted with a post, for example by commenting on it or 'liking' it

mom-monitored account – a social media account overseen by a parent

memer – someone who creates **memes**

memes – images with texts, usually humorous, that are copied and spread rapidly over social media

⭐ Boosting your vocabulary

Skilled writers choose their words with care. The activity below focuses on some key vocabulary in the source text, which has been highlighted on page 55.

Activity 2

a The writer tells the reader that they will 'discover' young adults starting a great career. Here are some synonyms for 'discover':

find   uncover   locate   dig up

learn   detect   bring to light   see

i Which synonym do you think is closest to 'discover' in this context? Explain why.

ii What connotations does the word 'discover' have that makes it sound exciting for readers?

b The writer describes the influencers as 'inspiring' and 'unique'. Here is a Frayer model exploring the word 'inspiring'.

Create your own Frayer model to explore the word 'unique'.

Frayer model

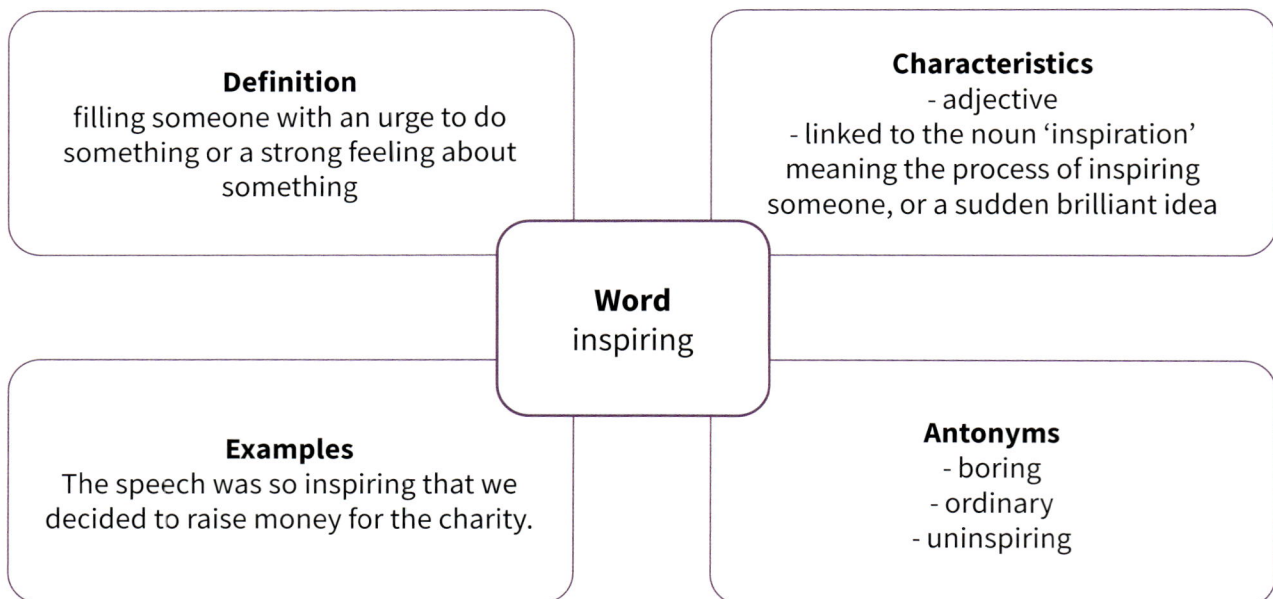

Definition
filling someone with an urge to do something or a strong feeling about something

Characteristics
- adjective
- linked to the noun 'inspiration' meaning the process of inspiring someone, or a sudden brilliant idea

Word
inspiring

Examples
The speech was so inspiring that we decided to raise money for the charity.

Antonyms
- boring
- ordinary
- uninspiring

Building your knowledge

The writer of the webpage uses **non-standard English** rather than **Standard English** to create a particular impression of both the agency and the teenage influencers it represents. Standard English is the formal style of English that is used in business and other official matters. Non-standard English is less formal and might be closer to how you speak with friends and family.

Key terms

abbreviation a shortened form of a word or phrase

colloquial suitable for ordinary conversation rather than formal speech or writing

non-standard English an informal version of English, often used with family and friends, including slang and regional variations

Standard English a widely recognised, formal version of English, not linked to any region, but used in schools, exams, official publications and in public announcements

Activity 3

a   The writer uses many **abbreviations** in the text. Find the abbreviations for the following terms:

details	direct message	collaboration

b   Why do you think the writer uses these abbreviations? What effect do they create for the reader?

Activity 4

a   The writer also expresses ideas in a **colloquial**, informal style. Match these informal words and phrases to their more formal expression.

Informal expressions

rock the looks too

hook up

early bird gets the worm

hacks

Formal expressions

quick and simple solutions

success comes to those who start work early

successfully wear the same outfits

connect or get in touch with

b   Look at this example of informal, non-standard English in the article: 'The only male to make our teen influencers list, Viraj is a master at the collab game.'

   i   Rewrite this sentence in more formal, Standard English.

   ii   Compare the Standard and non-standard English versions. Which is the most appropriate for the intended audience and purpose of the article?

Tip

Think about tone and level of familiarity.

The writer uses some other techniques to engage her audience and to maintain an informal, conversational, familiar tone.

Activity 5

a Look at the list of techniques below and find an example of each in the text on page 55. If you need a reminder of these techniques, refer back to previous units in Chapter 1 or the key terms glossary.

   i Direct address to the reader, using the **second person** pronoun 'you'

   ii Rhetorical questions to engage the reader

   iii **Exclamatory statements** to convey a sense of excitement

   iv Use of statistics to sound factually convincing

   v Variety of sentence lengths to create a sense of spontaneity and unpredictability

b Write a short paragraph explaining how the writer uses two of the language techniques listed above to create an engaging, informal tone for the target audience. Remember to include some quotations as examples.

> ## 🔑 Key terms
>
> **exclamatory statement** a sentence that expresses sudden or strong emotions, such as excitement. It usually ends with an exclamation mark
>
> **second person** a narrative voice that addresses the reader directly, using the pronoun 'you'

Activity 6

a Why do you think the writer uses non-standard English? What impact does she want to have on her readers? What does she want the reader to think, feel or imagine? Choose two of the statements below that you agree with.

> 'The writer does not know how to use Standard English.'

> 'The writer wants her writing to sound conversational, as though she is talking to the reader.'

> 'The writer wishes to sound like a teenager rather than someone older.'

> 'The writer uses non-standard English to make her writing appear exciting and full of energy.'

> 'The writer's audience would not expect her to use Standard English.'

b Write two short paragraphs to explain your points, including examples from the text. Try to link them to the text's overall purpose and intended audiences.

Putting it all together

In this unit, you have looked closely at an agency's website, and considered its purpose, language and intended audiences.

Activity 7

a Read the text extract below and the following question.

> The extract below comes from an article about teenage influencers. How does the writer use language to appeal to her intended audience and achieve her purpose?

Plan your response to this question, considering each of these points:

- who the writer's intended audience might be
- the writer's purpose and the effects she is trying to create
- the use of non-standard English, including abbreviations, colloquial expressions and rhetorical questions
- the vocabulary used to describe the young influencers.

b Now write your answer to the question above, considering your plan. Read this extract from one student's response to help you begin your answer.

> The extract includes non-standard English, for example, in the rhetorical question 'Can you believe what the Gen-Z kids are up to now?'. The colloquial phrase 'are up to' is used instead of 'are doing', as the writer wants to create a familiar, informal tone to engage the readers.

Best Teenager Influencers: 15 Teen Sensations You Must Follow on Social Media   by Bonita Brown

Can you believe what the **Gen-Z kids** are up to now?

Um, whatnot, you say?

This time it is something cool, we promise.

Let's see: they are remaking the celebrity brand!

5 Wait. What?

Gen-Z grew up with the Internet and social media like water for dolphins and they fashioned something out of it that we couldn't imagine – social media celebrities!

Be it Instagram, YouTube, or TikTok, these young people have carved out a **niche** for themselves, by building their own brands and dedicated followers among teenagers around the world.

10 They are being so successful, 'they deserve a shoutout' as they say on YouTube.

Gen-Z kids – Generation Z children (those born from mid 1990s to early 2010s)

niche – a specialised part of the market selling goods or services

2 TERROR AND WONDER

We all love to be excited, to have our emotions stirred and our imaginations fired up. Most of us enjoy the thrill of a scary movie or rollercoaster ride. After the thrill, comes the relief that we are safe but also the feeling that we witnessed something exciting. We also love to be awestruck by an amazing feat, a discovery or an invention. A sense of wonder can take us beyond the everyday, opening our imagination and intelligence to new ways of thinking and new possibilities.

Terror and wonder are powerful emotions that can be intertwined. Sometimes as something becomes more awesome, it can become terrifying, or the thrill of terror can be awesome.

In this chapter, you will explore how writers and speakers create terror and wonder for their audience; how they hint at forces more powerful than ourselves, or give us a thrilling glimpse of something new.

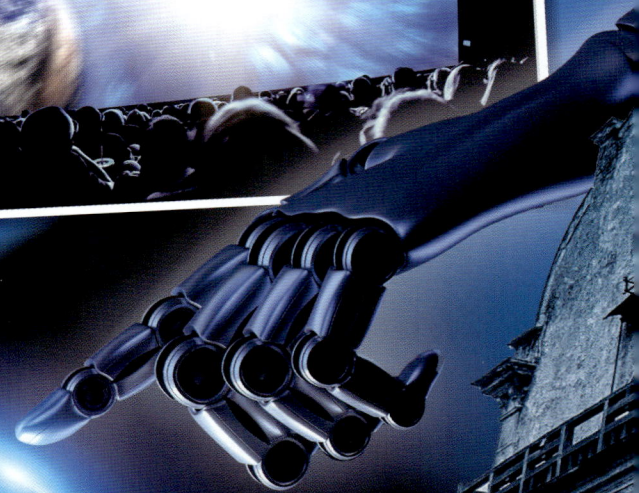

What makes us feel terrified? What makes us feel a sense of awe and wonder? Can the two feelings happen at the same time?

a   Look at the images numbered 1-6 on these pages. Decide how you feel about each one – terrified, amazed or do you feel a bit of both?

b   Select one image that you think best sums up the idea of terror. Imagine this image as a book cover. What would the title of your text be? What would the blurb say?

c   Select one image that you think best sums up the idea of wonder. Explain what aspects of the image make it awe-inspiring.

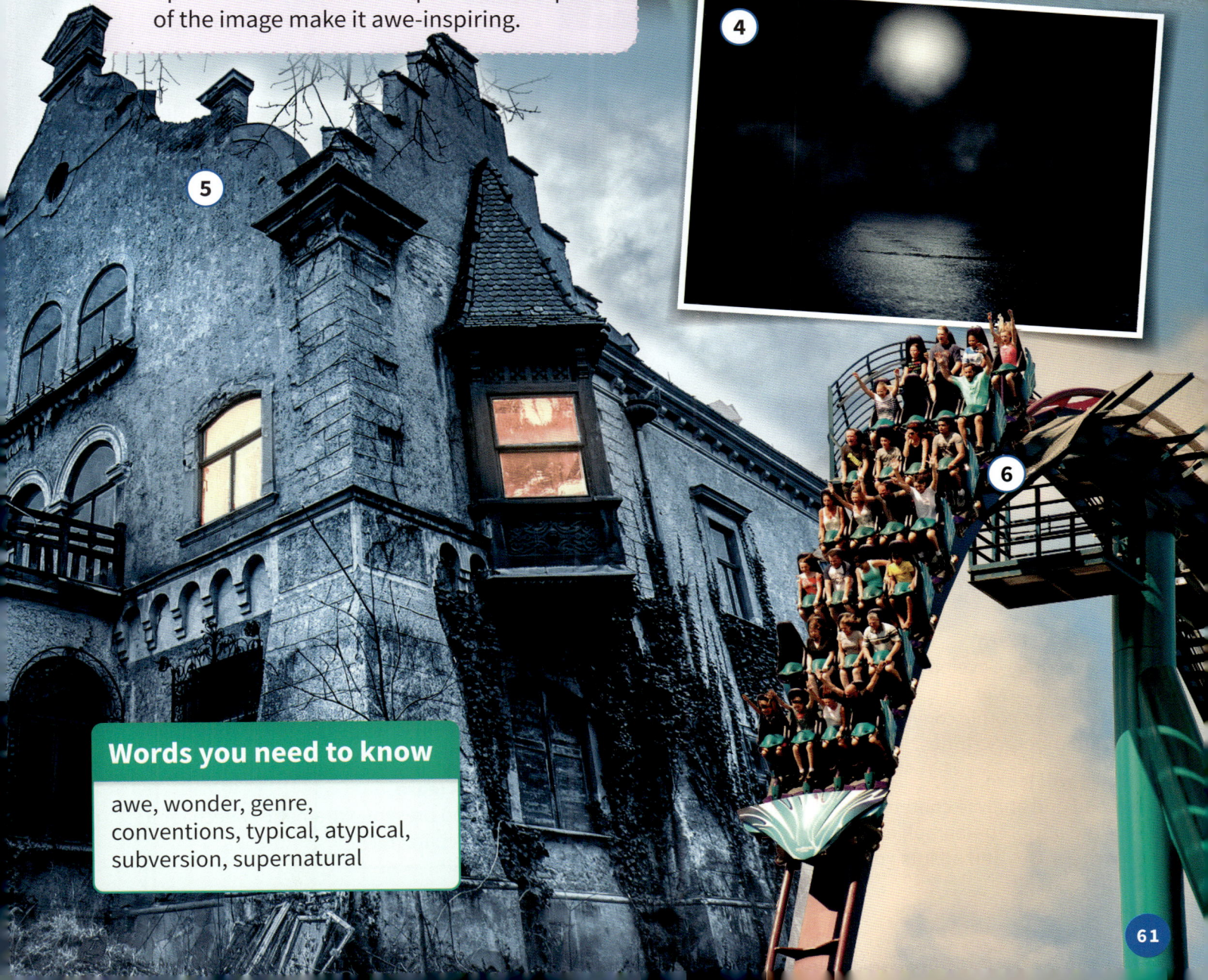

Words you need to know

awe, wonder, genre, conventions, typical, atypical, subversion, supernatural

2 Learning overview

This learning overview will show you where the chapter will take you on your learning journey. Use it to help you plan your learning, monitor what you have learned and then evaluate your knowledge.

2.1 What is gothic fiction? 64–69

Prepare
- What do you enjoy in a gothic story?

What I will learn
- The conventions of the gothic genre.
- How to identify and comment on features in a text.

How I will learn
- Examine how key conventions are applied in a range of texts.
- Write an analytical response to apply your understanding.

2.2 How can a setting create fear? 70–75

Prepare
- What places and settings make you feel uncomfortable?

What I will learn
- How writers create sinister settings using language techniques.
- How writers use structural techniques to build fear and apprehension.

How I will learn
- Examine the techniques writers use.
- Write the opening of a story, describing a sinister setting.

2.3 How do writers subvert a genre? 76–81

Prepare
- What would make somewhere frightening, like a spooky forest, suddenly appear safe and familiar?

What I will learn
- How writers develop and adapt genres, like the gothic, over time.
- The use of gothic conventions in contemporary stories.

How I will learn
- Read and analyse contemporary gothic texts.
- Write a short paragraph explaining how the writers uses and adapts gothic conventions in a text.

2.4 How is figurative language used to create fear? 82–87

Prepare
- Why do you think writers often include ghosts in stories and films?

What I will learn
- How dramatists make language choices to control the reaction of their audience.
- How figurative language and imagery can create fear and tension.

How I will learn
- Write and present a dramatic speech for a ghostly character.

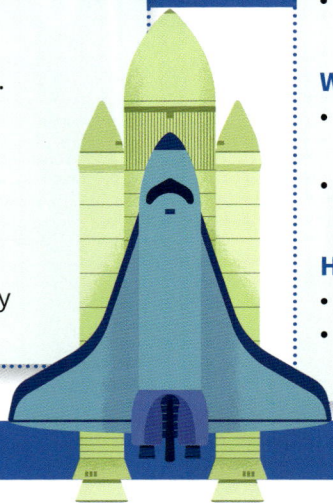

2.5 How do writers guide their readers?

88–93

Prepare
- Why would someone need a guide or advice text?

What I will learn
- How a guide can combine instructions and advice.
- How the structure and language features of a guide help to fulfil its purpose.

How I will learn
- Write a guide that includes instructions and advice.

2.6 How do writers provide explanation?

94–99

Prepare
- Do you think that robots are a good or bad idea, and why?

What I will learn
- How explanation and information can be combined in an article.
- How to explore the structure and language features of an explanation text.

How I will learn
- Write an analytical response about a writer's use of explanatory features in an article.

2.7 How do we compare texts?

100–105

Prepare
- Why might two writers write about the same topic in a different way?

What I will learn
- How to structure a comparison of two texts.
- How writers' choices of language, tone and register are shaped by purpose, audience and context.

How I will learn
- Write a comparative paragraph about two texts on the subject of AI.

2.8 How do writers present themselves?

106–111

Prepare
- What is more important: the facts of an event or a person's viewpoint of the event?

What I will learn
- How an autobiography can inform and entertain.
- The conventions of autobiographies, such as past tense, facts, opinions and description.

How I will learn
- Write an extract from your own autobiography.

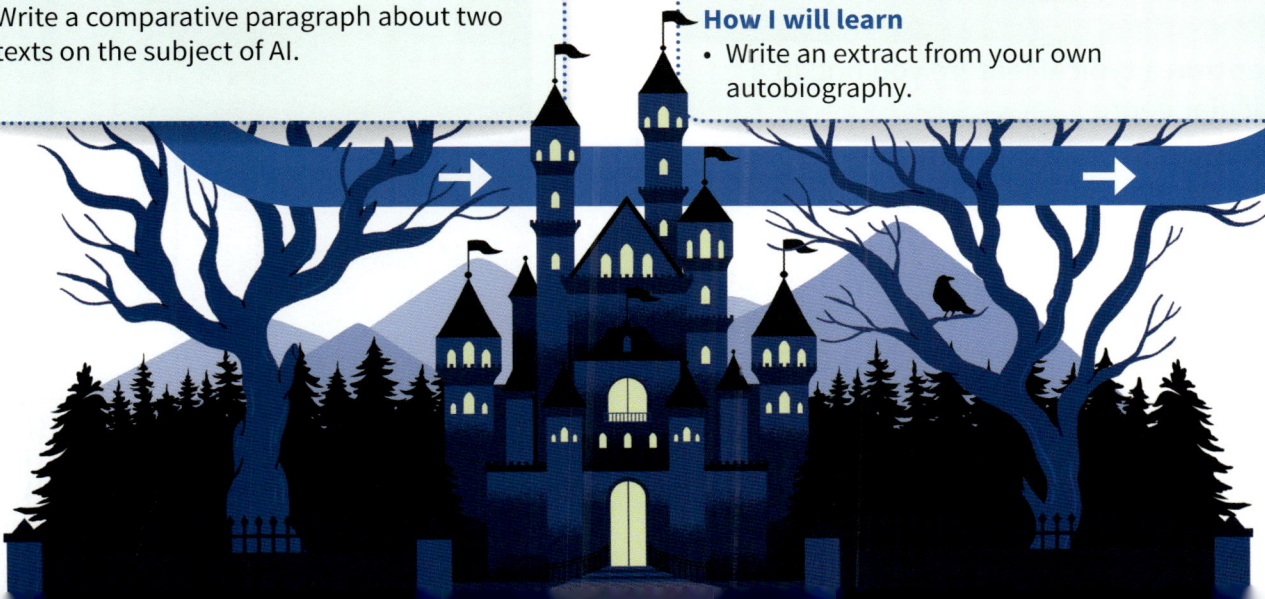

2.1 What is gothic fiction?

In this unit, you will:

- learn about the genre of gothic fiction
- explore how writers use the conventions of gothic fiction
- comment on the use of gothic conventions in a text.

What's the big idea?

Gothic literature first emerged in Europe in the 18th century but the ingredients of this style of writing are still popular today. It is a genre that creates intense emotions in the reader, such as terror and excitement as well as pleasure. Gothic conventions include mystery and fear, the supernatural, monstrous characters and haunted settings, where good and evil come into dramatic conflict.

In this unit, you will explore some of the conventions commonly linked to gothic fiction and learn how writers use them to create frightening yet thrilling effects for the reader.

⚙ Activity 1

a   Look carefully at the image on this page. Describe what you see, then think about the type of characters and plot you would associate with this image.

b   What gothic stories do you know? Think about dramas on television and film, as well as books.

🔑 Key terms

convention a typical feature you find in a particular genre

narrator a person who tells a story, especially in a book, play or film

the supernatural events and forces that cannot be explained by the known laws of nature or science

The short gothic story 'The Red Room' is set in an isolated castle. In the extract below, the **narrator** is determined to spend the night in a haunted room to disprove the existence of **the supernatural**. As you read this extract, look out for gothic **conventions**, such as the hint of supernatural forces and images of darkness versus light.

Extract from 'The Red Room' by H.G. Wells

"If," said I, "you will show me to this haunted room of yours, I will make myself comfortable there."

The old man with the cough jerked his head back so suddenly that it startled me, and shot another glance of his red eyes at me [...] but no one answered me. [...]

"This night of all nights!" said the old woman.

"Are you really going?" said the man, looking at me again for the third time, with that unnatural tilting of the face.

"It is what I came for," I said, and moved towards the door. As I did so, the old man rose and staggered round the table, so as to be closer to the others and to the fire. At the door I turned and looked at them, and saw they were all close together, dark against the firelight, staring at me over their shoulders, with an intent expression on their ancient faces.

"Good-night," I said, setting the door open.

"It's your own choosing," said the man.

I left the door wide open until the candle was well alight, and then I shut them in and walked down the chilly, echoing passage.

I must confess that the oddness of these three old pensioners in whose charge her ladyship had left the castle, and the deep-toned, old-fashioned furniture of the housekeeper's room in which they **foregathered**, affected me in spite of my efforts to keep myself at a matter-of-fact phase. They seemed to belong to another age, an older age, an age when things spiritual were different from this of ours, less certain; an age when omens and witches were credible, and ghosts beyond denying. Their very existence was spectral; the cut of their clothing, fashions born in dead brains. The ornaments and conveniences of the room about them were ghostly—the thoughts of vanished men, which still haunted rather than participated in the world of to-day. But with an effort I sent such thoughts to the right-about. The long, draughty **subterranean** passage was chilly and dusty, and my candle flared and made the shadows cower and quiver. The echoes rang up and down the spiral staircase, and a shadow came sweeping up after me, and one fled before me into the darkness overhead. I came to the landing and stopped there for a moment, listening to a rustling that I fancied I heard; then, satisfied of the absolute silence, I pushed open the **baize**-covered door and stood in the corridor.

---

foregathered – assembled or gathered together
subterranean – underground

baize – thick green woollen cloth, often used to cover snooker and card tables

⭐ Boosting your vocabulary

Skilled writers choose their words with care. The activity below explores some of the vocabulary used in the source text, which has been highlighted on page 65.

Activity 2

a 'Spectral' means ghostly. Consider the following sentence: 'We felt a spectral presence in the room.'

   i Give two details of what might be occurring in the room to make it feel 'spectral'. For example, how might the air feel?

   ii Write a sentence using the word 'spectral' and the details you have suggested above.

b The narrator refers to a time when 'omens and witches were credible'. The word 'credible' means believable. Read the words below. Some of these are **synonyms** of credible. Which word is not?

    plausible   trustworthy   inconceivable   possible

c The inhabitants of the castle are described as having 'ancient faces'. The word 'ancient' means belonging to the past. It suggests that the inhabitants come from another time and place, building a picture that they are 'otherworldly'. Choose two other words you could use to describe them that would have a similar effect.

❓ Did you know?

Some people believe that the gothic genre began with a novel called *The Castle of Otranto*, written by Horace Walpole in 1764. It is set in a medieval castle that is cursed with an ancient prophecy predicting the tragic death of everyone who lives there.

🔑 Key terms

genre a type of story, e.g. *horror*, *romance*, *adventure*, *science fiction*

synonym a word or phrase that means the same, or almost the same, as another word or phrase

💡 Building your knowledge

Gothic stories use many of the same conventions, all of which help to create a powerful, often terrifying story. Readers can enjoy feeling the thrill of fear experienced by the characters, without experiencing danger themselves.

One of the key conventions in the gothic **genre** is the presence of supernatural forces, such as ghosts. This often suggests that the past is somehow lingering in the present, with a malevolent intent (evil purpose). This creates a sense of fear in the characters and for the reader.

Activity 3

a   Look at lines 1–3. What word does the narrator use to describe the room where he intends to stay? How does it suggest the influence of the past on the present?

b   How do the responses of the inhabitants show their fear, creating **tension** for the reader?

Another key convention in the gothic genre is the presence of a monstrous character. This character is often described as being unnatural or alien in some way. In the extract, the three older characters who live in the castle are described as grotesque and unnatural. Instead of portraying these older people as wise and safe, the writer suggests that they do not really belong in this time or place.

Activity 4

What details can you find in the description of the 'three old pensioners' that hint at their unusual, fearsome qualities? Think about their appearance as well as their behaviour. Complete a spider diagram like the one started below.

unnatural tilt of the face — **'three old pensioners'** — red eyes

Most gothic stories are set in ancient, isolated places, which lack the security and comfort of the modern world. The action often takes place at night, or in gloomy settings, where darkness makes things feel mysterious and characters seem vulnerable. In literature, darkness is used as a **symbol** for nighttime and the unknown, whereas light is used to represent daylight, therefore safety and hope.

Activity 5

a   What two sources of light does the writer describe in the extract?

b   How does the writer use them to suggest comfort and safety?

c   How does the writer make the darkness and shadows seem threatening for the narrator?

> ### 🔑 Key terms
>
> **symbol** something specific that represents a more general quality or situation
>
> **tension** a feeling of being on edge with nerves stretched tight

Activity 6

Use what you have learned to write some short responses to each of the questions below. Use some of the sentence starters to help you.

a   How does the writer use gothic conventions in the setting of the extract?

> The idea of the supernatural is introduced in the first lines of the extract, when the writer describes…

b   How does the writer use images of light and darkness in the passage?

> The writer features two sources of light in the extract… In contrast…

c   How does the description of the 'three old pensioners' add to the unnerving atmosphere in this extract?

> The three elderly people represent a subversive form of the 'monster' character in gothic convention. The writer hints at their unusualness by…

⬆ Stretch yourself

Frankenstein is a novel written by Mary Shelley but the story has been retold in many different forms. From your general knowledge of the story, what classic gothic conventions does it use?

🧩 Putting it all together

In this unit, you have learned about the genre of gothic fiction and some of its key conventions. You will now read an extract from another gothic novel and explore how this writer uses gothic conventions to excite, thrill and frighten readers.

In the extract opposite, Jonathan Harker, who has arrived at Dracula's castle in Transylvania, is about to meet the Count for the first time.

Extract from *Dracula* by Bram Stoker

I heard a heavy step approaching behind the great door, and saw through the chinks the gleam of a coming light. Then there was the sound of rattling chains and the clanking of massive bolts drawn back. A key was turned with the loud grating noise of long disuse, and the great door swung back.

Within stood a tall old man, clean shaven save for a long white moustache, and clad in black

5 from head to foot, without a single speck of colour about him anywhere. He held in his hand an antique silver lamp, in which the flame burned without a chimney or globe of any kind, throwing long quivering shadows as it flickered in the draught of the open door. The old man motioned me in with his right hand with a courtly gesture, saying in excellent English, but with a strange intonation, "Welcome to my house! Enter freely and of your own free will!" He made no motion of

10 stepping to meet me, but stood like a statue, as though his gesture of welcome had fixed him into stone. The instant, however, that I had stepped over the threshold, he moved impulsively forward, and holding out his hand grasped mine with a strength which made me wince, an effect which was not lessened by the fact that it seemed cold as ice, more like the hand of a dead than a living man.

Activity 7

Now answer this question, following the steps below.

> How does Stoker use gothic conventions in the extract to create a sense of mystery and fear?

Step 1: Look for evidence of the following gothic conventions in the text:
- the supernatural
- monstrous characters
- isolated/haunted locations
- darkness versus light.

Step 2: Note down the effect of these conventions on the reader. How do they make you feel and why?

Step 3: Write your response in full, using your notes to help you. Below are some sentence starters to use.

The passage begins with a focus on…

The description of the character focuses on…

One of the most striking conventions is the use of…

The writer creates a sense of mystery and fear by…

2.2 How can a setting create fear?

In this unit, you will:

- learn how writers create sinister settings
- explore the use of language and structural techniques to build fear and tension
- write the opening of a story describing a sinister setting.

What's the big idea?

In some stories, the anticipation of what might be going to happen is more frightening than the events themselves. Creative writers and film producers spend a lot of time carefully constructing a sinister setting so that the audience has plenty of clues that something terrible is about to happen and is anxiously waiting for the drama to unfold. The suspense and tension creates a thrilling mix of excitement and fear.

In this unit, you will look at how writers generate fear through the creation of a sinister setting. You will explore how a writer chooses language carefully to create a sense of unease and apprehension, and uses structure to build up a sense of looming danger and menace.

Activity 1

a What things do people find scary? Think about the dark or spiders. What sort of places are often depicted as making people uneasy, and why?

b Discuss stories or films that have come across as frightening. Which elements are the most scary or cause the most **suspense**? For example, the setting, characters or events that happened?

? Did you know?

The word 'sinister', suggesting harm or evil, comes from the Latin word *sinistra* meaning 'on the left'. Traditionally the left side of things was thought to be unlucky.

🔑 Key term

suspense a feeling of anxious uncertainty while waiting for something to happen or become known

The extract below is from the thriller novel *Fog Island* by Mariette Lindstein. It describes how the inhabitants of Eastwood Island experience the arrival of a mysterious fog.

Extract from *Fog Island* by Mariette Lindstein

The night before had been a clear night. Stars appeared as studded diamonds into **swathes** of thick black velvet. However, the rising sun brought with it a cloak of grey fuzz, dousing the island's hills in a milky mist, hiding the tops of the mountains from view. School children filed off to the one school in the town, giggling as they waved their hands in front
5 of their faces, **feigning** blindness. The mist turned in on itself, folded and creased, layers wrapped around layers until the **opaque white tulle** turned cotton grey. The soup sat stagnant. Dead air. Suffocating.

Eastwood Island was an isolated community, cut off from the mainland by a huge expanse of water. No power lines could run through the water, forcing it to be entirely independent:
10 Eastwood Island ran its own **generator**, phone lines, and gas mains. By two o'clock the schools were forced to close. The older children whooped and screeched, invigorated by the freedom; the younger ones whimpered and sobbed, unsteady with uncertainty. By the time they arrived home, the power was out. Switching on radios, mainland channels barely crackled through, but the Island based stations had been abandoned. Then when the
15 time came to cook the evening meal, ovens were turned on, only to be turned off again. No gas. And then no phones. The adults muttered excuses about the fog interfering with the generator; this made no sense (and they knew it) but it somehow **assuaged** their own fears to agree upon a reason, no matter how **fictitious**. Outside, the fog sat like an unwelcome guest, lounging heavily across the landscape of rolling fields and small hilltops. Its overstuffed,
20 bloated clouds spilling into the next meadow and then the next, and then the next. Night fell. Morning came. But the fog was still there. And the following day. And the following week.

---

swathes – broad strips
feigning – pretending
opaque white tulle – non-transparent fine white cloth

generator – a machine which produces electricity
assuaged – soothed and reduced
fictitious – imagined or unreal

Activity 2

a What do the children think of the fog in the opening paragraph?

b How do the inhabitants of Eastwood Island react differently as the day progresses and the fog gets thicker? Give two examples.

c Why do the adults say the fog has interfered with the generator?

⭐ Boosting your vocabulary

Skilled writers choose their words with care. The activity below explores some of the vocabulary used in the source text, which has been highlighted on page 71.

Activity 3

a To 'douse' means to throw water or another liquid on something. In the extract, the grey fuzz is 'dousing' the island's hills in a milky mist'. The combination of the word 'dousing' and the **noun phrase** 'milky mist' makes the action seem quite gentle and harmless.

Choose one word from the list below that could replace 'dousing' and still have that unthreatening **tone**.

   drenching   soaking   saturating   drizzling

   sprinkling   coating   covering

b Later in the paragraph, the fog is described as 'suffocating', which means that it is stopping the inhabitants from breathing. What has happened to the tone of the text?

c The word 'stagnant' means that something is not flowing or running. Stagnant water can smell unpleasant and dirty. The writer creates a striking image in the **metaphor** 'The soup sat stagnant'.

   i What does the image of the 'soup' represent?

   ii What senses is the writer appealing to?

   iii What does this metaphor suggest about the mist?

✅ Tip

Remember that the tone of a piece of writing can change within a text, gradually changing the reader's response to an event, character or place.

🗝 Key terms

metaphor a comparison that says one thing is something else, e.g. *Amy was a rock*

noun phrase a noun plus information before and/or after the noun

simile a comparison of one thing to another, using as or like, e.g. *He swam like a fish*

tone the writer's feeling or attitude expressed towards their subject

Building your knowledge

Writers use language and structural techniques to direct and stir up the reader's ideas and emotions. These techniques might include:

juxtaposition   contrast   figurative language   foreshadowing   cliffhanger

Activity 4

Match the techniques above to the correct definitions below.

words or phrases with a meaning that is different from the literal meaning, including **similes** and metaphors

a technique that gives a hint or warning about something that will develop later, e.g. a dramatic thunderstorm starts before something dangerous happens

an exciting event or idea at the end of a section of text, leaving the reader eager to know what happens next, e.g. a climber feels the ground shudder and hears the roar of an approaching avalanche at the end of a chapter

the difference between two or more things; also, to compare or show a difference

putting words, ideas or images together to show a contrast or relationship between them, e.g. *the manager's expression changed from sweet to sour*

Now look at how the author of *Fog Island* uses these techniques in the first paragraph of the extract. Imagine you are the author, jotting down thoughts as you describe the setting below.

The night before had been a clear night. Stars appeared as studded diamonds into swathes of thick black velvet. However, the rising sun brought with it a cloak of grey fuzz, dousing the island's hills in a milky mist, hiding the tops of the mountains from view. School children filed off to the one school in the town, giggling as they waved their hands in front of their faces, feigning blindness. The mist turned in on itself, folded and creased, layers wrapped around layers until the opaque white tulle turned cotton grey. The soup sat stagnant. Dead air. Suffocating.

This suggests that something dramatic has happened. The sentence is deliberately short and in the past tense, and contrasts the night with the previous night.

The author uses figurative language to show a contrast: she has juxtaposed 'diamonds' with 'cloak of grey fuzz'.

The image of the pretty 'tulle' material turning to a dull 'cotton grey' foreshadows a more sinister event to come.

The use of three short sentences that get shorter and more threatening leaves the opening paragraph on a cliffhanger.

Activity 5

Read lines 1–3 of the extract from *Fog Island* again.

Consider how the writer **juxtaposes** earlier and later events, drawing out the contrast. This contrast builds tension by suggesting that a normal, positive time has now passed and that something negative is about to replace it.

Using the same structure, complete the opening sentences below, creating a clear feeling that everything has now changed.

> The morning before had been… However, …
>
> The afternoon before had been… However, …

You could use some of the words below or choose your own.

bright   bustling   vibrant   cheerful

sparkling   thrilling   optimistic

Key term

juxtapose to put words, ideas or images together to show a contrast or relationship between them

Activity 6

Imagine you are planning a story about some friends who become lost in a strange forest. How might you foreshadow this event earlier in the story? Note down two ideas. Here is one student's idea.

> One of the characters could be shown always losing their phone, glasses or inhaler.

Activity 7

Using your knowledge of structural and language techniques, discuss what you think the writer is trying to achieve in the second paragraph of the extract. How is the writer building up tension and suspense?

Tip

Think about what has come before (the sequence of events) and how this adds to or changes the feelings of the reader.

Putting it all together

Activity 8

Now plan and write the opening of your own story, starting with a description of a sinister setting. Use the extract from *Fog Island* as a style model and follow the steps below.

Step 1: Choose one of your sentences from Activity 5. Remember that the idea of something 'frightening' can come from the unexpected.

Step 2: Note down key ideas for your description and consider how you can use some of the language and structural techniques you have learned about:

- short sentences
- figurative language
- juxtaposition
- contrast
- foreshadowing
- cliffhangers.

Step 3: Plan the overall structure of your description of the setting. For example:

Paragraph 1: Include an engaging opening, for example: 'The night before had been a clear night…'

Paragraph 2: Introduce the setting with details of what it is usually like and use contrast to show how it has changed.

Paragraph 3: Zoom in further on the changed situation. Use foreshadowing to hint that it will become worse.

Paragraph 4: End with a cliffhanger.

Step 4: Draft your key sentences that showcase where you have used specific techniques. For example:

> Before there was laughter and joy. However, now all that could be found was silence.

This is my example of contrast and I will use it in paragraph 2.

Step 5: Write out your story opening in full. Remember to choose your vocabulary carefully in order to create the effects you want for your reader.

Stretch yourself

Review your work. Try to edit it and add to it, to increase the level of fear and terror!

2.3 How do writers subvert a genre?

In this unit, you will:

- learn how writers subvert and adapt genres over time
- explore the use of gothic conventions in contemporary stories
- comment on how a writer subverts gothic conventions to create fear and tension.

What's the big idea?

Many of the original gothic stories were set in remote places such as abandoned castles and crumbling manor houses. These isolated settings added to the vulnerability of the characters. However, as society became more industrial in the 19th and 20th centuries, more gothic stories were set in towns and cities. These urban spaces triggered new fears, such as rising levels of crime, industrial pollution and suspicions of new scientific advances. Writers showed how terror can lurk not at a distance, but close to home – even within ourselves!

In this unit, you will explore how the genre of gothic fiction has changed over time, with writers adapting and subverting some of the conventions, giving them a modern twist.

Activity 1

Think back to some of the gothic conventions covered in Unit 1. For example:

- monstrous characters
- gloomy settings
- hauntings
- curses
- the supernatural
- conflict between good and evil.

a What modern stories do you know that use some of these conventions? Think about stories in films and on television, as well as in comics and novels.

b Have any of the gothic conventions been **subverted** in these examples?

Key term

subvert to change an established way something is done

Did you know?

Robert Louis Stevenson's *The Strange Case of Dr Jekyll and Mr Hyde* includes gothic conventions that have been subverted. For example, the story was set in London at the time it was written, which is familiar, rather than a gloomy, remote setting in the past. Stevenson also includes a monstrous character, Mr Hyde, but subverts it by including it as the alternate personality of a sensitive character, Dr Jekyll.

The extract below is from the first book in the *Twilight* series by Stephenie Meyer. The story is set in Forks, a remote town in America. In this extract, the narrator, Bella, is leaving her home in sunny Phoenix to stay with her father in Forks.

Extract from *Twilight* by Stephenie Meyer

My mother drove me to the airport with the windows rolled down. It was seventy-five degrees in Phoenix, the sky a perfect, cloudless blue. I was wearing my favourite shirt – sleeveless, white **eyelet** lace; I was wearing it as a farewell gesture. My
5 carry-on item was a **parka**.

In the Olympic Peninsula of northwest Washington State, a small town named Forks exists under a near-constant cover of clouds. It rains on this inconsequential town more than any other place in the United States of America. It was from
10 this town and its gloomy, omnipresent shade that my mother escaped with me when I was only a few months old. It was in this town that I'd been compelled to spend a month every summer until I was fourteen. That was the year I finally put my foot down; these past three summers, my dad, Charlie,
15 **vacationed** with me in California for two weeks instead.

It was to Forks that I now exiled myself – an action that I took with great horror. I detested Forks. I loved Phoenix. I loved the sun and the blistering heat. I loved the vigorous, sprawling city.

eyelet – patterns of small holes in a fabric
parka – a heavy winter coat with a hood, traditionally lined with fur
vacationed – took holidays

Later in the novel, Bella gives us the following description:

Thick fog was all I could see out my window in the morning, and I could feel the **claustrophobia** creeping up on me. You could never see the sky here; it was like a cage.

claustrophobia – fear of enclosed small spaces

★ Boosting your vocabulary

Skilled writers choose their words with care. The activity below explores some of the vocabulary used in the source text, which has been highlighted on page 77.

Activity 2

a The town of Forks is described as 'inconsequential', which means that it is not important. What does this suggest Bella feels about her new home?

b This extract includes a sense of foreboding, that something bad is about to happen. The word 'omnipresent' means something that is everywhere.

   i Explain how this word adds to this feeling about the setting.

   ii The **prefix** 'omni-' comes from the Latin word *omnis* meaning 'all'. Think of another word that starts with the prefix 'omni-' and explain its meaning.

c Complete the following Frayer model for the word 'vigorous'.

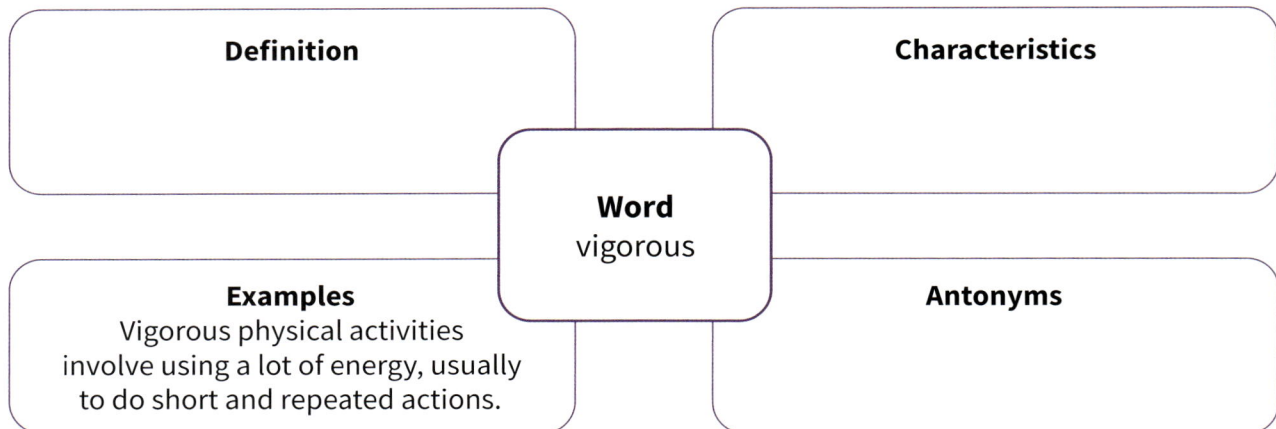

Definition	Characteristics
Word vigorous	
Examples Vigorous physical activities involve using a lot of energy, usually to do short and repeated actions.	**Antonyms**

d How do all the words combine to emphasise the oppressive and menacing atmosphere of Forks compared with 'vigorous' Phoenix?

🔑 Key terms

antonym a word that has the opposite meaning of a particular word

prefix a word or group of letters placed in front of another word to add to or change its meaning

💡 Building your knowledge

Subverting a genre means to include conventions that adapt or go against what would be typically be expected in that genre. For example, the setting of a gothic story might be in a bright or public place, rather than a gloomy, remote place. Writers do this for impact: it will unsettle and engage the reader, as they can no longer predict what is going to happen.

In the extract, Meyer creates a typical gothic atmosphere, but she subverts it by setting it in a small town called Forks, rather than in a single building in an isolated place. Forks is described as a 'small' and 'inconsequential' town and although the location might not be isolated, there are hints that Bella will feel lonely and cut off there.

Activity 3

Annotate this quotation to show how it suggests that Bella will be lonely and cut off from the world. Think about the use of the word 'escaped' and the connotations of the phrase 'gloomy, omnipresent shade'.

'It was from this town and its gloomy, omnipresent shade that my mother escaped with me when I was only a few months old.'

Meyer also subverts the otherworldly conventions of the gothic genre by setting *Twilight* in contemporary times and including modern features, such as transport. Bella travels to Forks by car and plane, which makes it more believable yet unsettling for the reader, as it suggests that Bella is travelling back there willingly, despite knowing the type of place that it is.

Activity 4

a Remind yourself of the other gothic conventions covered in Unit 1. Which of these has also been subverted in the *Twilight* extract?

b Write a sentence to explain how it subverts the conventions of the gothic genre.

✅ Tip

Remember that subverts is another way of saying adapts or changes.

There is no direct description of a monster or the supernatural, but the writer uses **figurative language**, such as **personification** and simile to suggest larger forces are beginning to work against Bella. Remember that personification can make an idea or thing have living qualities, for example leaves can 'dance' in the wind.

Activity 5

Look at the second extract on page 77, taken from later in the novel.

a The writer uses personification in the phrase 'claustrophobia creeping up on me'. What is the effect of the word 'creeping' in this sentence?

b What does the simile 'it was like a cage' suggest about Bella's feelings?

As well as including and subverting gothic conventions, Meyer uses some of the structural techniques explored in Unit 2. The purpose of these is also to create a sense of unease and fear for the reader. For example, images of sunny, 'vigorous', hot and thriving Phoenix are juxtaposed with the gloom, rain and dullness in Forks. This physical contrast foreshadows the frightening dangers Bella will soon face.

Activity 6

The novel goes on to introduce vampires and supernatural events. Is this something we can tell might happen from this opening or not?

🧩 Putting it all together

You are now going to use what you have learned about how writers adapt gothic conventions to modern stories by commenting on another text.

Read the extract from *A Monster Calls* opposite and answer the questions in Activity 7.

🔑 Key terms

figurative language words or phrases with a meaning that is different from the literal meaning

personification showing something non-human as having human characteristics

Activity 7

a What gothic conventions can you identify in this text? Look back to page 76 if you need a reminder of these conventions.

b The tree is a yew tree. How is this important in linking to gothic conventions?

c How does the writer subvert gothic conventions?

d Write a short paragraph explaining how the writer uses and subverts gothic conventions in this extract.

> ✅ **Tip**
>
> Think about Conor's reaction to the monster and the setting.

Extract from A Monster Calls by Patrick Ness

A cloud moved in front of the moon, covering the whole landscape in darkness, and a *whoosh* of wind rushed down the hill and into his room, billowing the curtains. He heard the creaking and cracking of wood again, groaning like a living thing, like the hungry stomach of the world growling for a meal.

Then the cloud passed, and the moon shone again.

5 On the **yew tree**.

Which now stood firmly in the middle of his back garden.

And here was the monster.

As Conor watched, the uppermost branches of the tree gathered themselves into a great and terrible face, shimmering into a mouth and nose and even eyes, peering back at him. Other
10 branches twisted around one another, always creaking, always groaning, until they formed two long arms and a second leg to set down beside the main trunk. The rest of the tree gathered itself into a spine and then a **torso**, the thin, needle-like leaves weaving together to make a green, furry skin that moved and breathed as if there were muscles and lungs underneath. [...]

And then the monster spoke. [...]

15 *I have come to get you, Conor O'Malley*, the monster said, pushing against the house, shaking the pictures off Conor's wall, sending books and electronic gadgets and an old stuffed toy rhino tumbling to the floor. [...]

But Conor didn't run.

In fact, he found he wasn't even frightened.

20 All he could feel, all he *had* felt since the monster revealed itself, was a growing disappointment.

Because this wasn't the monster he was expecting.

"So come and get me then," he said.

---

yew tree – type of tree commonly found in churchyards and said to purify the dead as they entered the underworld in Greek mythology

torso – the trunk (central part) of a human body

2.4 How is figurative language used to create fear?

In this unit, you will:

- learn how dramatists use language to control the reaction of their audience
- explore how figurative language, including imagery, can create fear and tension
- write and present a dramatic speech for a ghostly character.

What's the big idea?

Since Ancient Greek times, ghosts have featured in dramas. They often play a key role in the plot, revealing terrible secrets, urging characters to act, or haunting those with a guilty conscience. Their presence is an unsettling reminder that all life comes to an end.

In this unit, you will look at how a ghostly character in William Shakespeare's play *Hamlet* generates terror through his use of figurative language and imagery.

Activity 1

a The idea of ghosts often inspires writers. Discuss any ghost stories that you know of. They might be films, books or television programmes. What sort of feelings and reactions do these create for their audience?

b Write a simile or metaphor based on the ghostly image on this page. You could either describe the scene or someone's reaction to it.

✔ Tip

Remember that stories can create a mix of emotions in the reader or audience.

In the following extract, the ghost of Hamlet's father tells Hamlet that he has been murdered and urges his son to take revenge.

Extract from *Hamlet* Act 1 Scene 5 by William Shakespeare

Ghost: I am thy father's spirit,
Doomed for a certain term to walk the night,
And for the day confined to fast in fires,
Till the foul crimes done in my days of nature

5   Are burnt and purged away. But that I am forbid
To tell the secrets of my prison house,
I could a tale unfold whose lightest word
Would **harrow up** thy soul, freeze thy young blood,
Make thy two eyes like stars **start from** their **spheres**,

10   Thy knotted and combinèd **locks** to part,
And each particular hair to stand on end
Like quills upon the fretful **porpentine**.
But this eternal blazon must not be
To ears of flesh and blood. **List**, list, O, list!

15   If thou didst ever thy dear father love
[...]
Revenge his foul and most **unnatural** murder.

Hamlet: Murder!

Ghost: Murder most foul, as in the best it is,

20   But this most foul, strange and unnatural.

Hamlet: Haste me to know't, that I with wings as swift
As **meditation** or the thoughts of love
May sweep to my revenge.

Ghost: [...]

25   'Tis given out that, sleeping in my orchard,
A serpent stung me. So the whole ear of Denmark
Is by a **forgèd process** of my death
Rankly abused. But know, thou noble youth,
The serpent that did sting thy father's life

30   Now wears his crown.

The ghost has no peace and is forced to walk all night and burn in fires as a punishment for his sins.

The ghost urges Hamlet to act on his behalf and take revenge for his murder.

The ghost reveals his killer was Hamlet's uncle, who is now king.

---

harrow up – torment, or inflict pain
start from – fall out of
spheres – (eye) sockets; also orbits
locks – locks or strands of hair
porpentine – porcupine

list – listen
unnatural – going against natural family bonds
meditation – thoughts
forgèd process – false account

Activity 2

What gothic conventions can you recognise in this extract from *Hamlet*?
Look back to Unit 1 to remind yourself of the conventions of the gothic genre.

★ Boosting your vocabulary

Skilled writers choose their words with care. The activity below explores some of the vocabulary used in the source text, which has been highlighted on page 83.

Activity 3

a The word 'doomed' in this extract refers to the idea of being forced to do something. The ghost is 'doomed' to walk the earth until Hamlet can get revenge for his death. Consider the following synonyms for 'doomed' and select the one you feel has the most powerful, haunting impact. Explain the reason for your choice.

   sentenced   condemned   punished   damned   destined

b The ghost is condemned to suffer until his 'foul crimes' are 'purged away'. A synonym for 'purge' is to 'cleanse'. The ghost wants to be washed clean of his sins so that he can rest in peace. Use the word 'purge' in a sentence of your own.

c If you take 'revenge' you want to hurt or punish someone who has hurt you. Look at the list of words below and decide which one suggests the 'weakest' effect and which one is the 'strongest'. Imagine using the word in the sentence:

   revenge   repayment   compensation   justice   vengeance

   Hamlet wants to gain _____ for his murdered father.

Place the words on a scale from weakest on the left to strongest on the right.

   1   5   10

Building your knowledge

Shakespeare's use of powerful figurative language, including vivid **imagery**, are part of what makes him one of the greatest playwrights. In this extract, we can explore his use of metaphors, similes and symbols and how they build up the sense of horror for the audience.

Shakespeare cleverly controls the audience's emotions in lines 5–14 by describing how they would react if they knew the detail of the ghost's punishments. The ghost uses a metaphor to describe the effects of his 'tale', which he says would 'freeze thy young blood'. This suggests that the horror is so great that it would paralyse and kill someone like extreme cold. We often associate fear with a sense of coldness.

Key terms

extended metaphor a long metaphor which builds up an image in detail over many lines

imagery language that creates pictures in the reader's mind

Activity 4

a What metaphor does Shakespeare use in line 9 to describe what would happen to a listener's eyes if they heard the ghost's tale? How does this add to the sense of horror?

b Shakespeare also uses a simile in this line. What is it and how does it make the image more powerful?

c In lines 10–12, Shakespeare uses an **extended metaphor** to describe the effects of terror. An extended metaphor can build up an image over many sentences or even paragraphs. It keeps adding to the basic image, making it more powerful for the audience or reader. Describe the effect of the extended metaphor Shakespeare uses in this extract. (Think of the modern expression of fear making your 'hair stand on end'.)

d Draw a simple sketch of the image that Shakespeare is creating and annotate it using quotations from the speech.

e Write your own simile and metaphor to describe the experience of a terrified person. Use the sentence starters below or your own.

I was so scared that my whole body…

Her face looked like…

The ghost refers to his killer as a 'serpent' (snake) who is now wearing his crown. The image of a snake is powerful because snakes are often seen as a symbol for negative ideas. They have **connotations** of undesirable qualities such as slyness, dishonesty and temptation.

Activity 5

a   A crown can also be a symbol. What does it represent?

b   What other creature does Hamlet refer to in lines 21–23? How does this reference help to build up a sense of urgency?

c   Write a sentence describing someone using animal imagery, suggesting qualities that are often associated with that animal. For example:

> Her wolfish eyes focused on the tray of puddings.

Shakespeare builds up a sense of urgency and danger through his use of **rhetorical devices** in this speech, as well as through figurative language.

Activity 6

Find examples of the following rhetorical devices in the extract and explain how they add to the sense of drama and power of the ghost's speech.

- **Repetition**
- **Emotive language**
- **Imperative** (command)

🔑 Key terms

connotation an idea or feeling linked to a word, as well as its main meaning

emotive language word choices that create a strong emotional reaction in the audience or reader

imperative a sentence that gives an order, command or instruction

repetition using the same word or phrase more than once

rhetorical device a language feature that has a persuasive or impressive effect on listeners and readers

✅ Tip

Look back at pages 12–17 to remind yourself of these rhetorical devices.

⬆ Stretch yourself

What stories do you know that feature snakes? Think about traditional tales, myths and legends, as well as films and novels today. What characteristics are associated with snakes? Are they generally good or bad characters?

Activity 7

Imagine you are an actor playing the part of Hamlet's father's ghost. With a partner talk about how you would present this speech to bring fear to the audience. Discuss:

- how the ghost might look
- how the ghost might move and what **gestures** and facial expressions it might use
- how you would deliver the speech for most impact, thinking about tone of voice, **pace**, volume and where to pause.

🔑 Key terms

gesture using your hands to indicate meaning, e.g. to help emphasise certain points

pace the speed at which someone speaks or moves or something happens

🧩 Putting it all together

Activity 8

✏️ You have explored how Shakespeare uses figurative language imagery and rhetorical devices to present a terrifying speech for audiences of *Hamlet*. Now you are going to write and present your own ghostly speech, using the knowledge and skills you have gained.

Follow the steps below.

Step 1: Decide on the identity of your ghost, who it is addressing and why.

⬇

Step 2: Make notes on what your ghost will say and how it will bring terror to the scene. It may describe a horrible murder, or the punishments it is suffering.

⬇

Step 3: Think carefully about using figurative language (metaphors, similes and symbols) to conjure up vivid, frightening pictures in the audience's mind.

⬇

Step 4: If your ghost is trying to persuade another character to do something, decide on some rhetorical devices to make the demand urgent, dangerous and dramatic.

⬇

Step 5: When you are happy with your speech, practise delivering it to make maximum impact on your audience.

✅ Tip

Remember that you are writing a speech from the ghost's point of view, so you will need to use the first-person pronoun 'I'.

2.5 How do writers guide their readers?

In this unit, you will:

- learn how a guide can combine instructions and advice
- explore how the structure and language features of a guide help to fulfil its purpose
- write a guide of your own, including instructions and advice.

What's the big idea?

Instruction texts tell people what to do. They may consist of rules or give step-by-step teaching on how to make or do something. Advice texts give readers information and suggest choices that the reader could make.

In this unit, you will focus on a guide to the wonders of stargazing (looking at the stars on a clear night). You will explore how the writer uses a combination of instructions and advice in the text to guide the reader through the process of stargazing.

Activity 1

a When did you last read instructions? What were they for and where were they?

b Where have you found instructions?

c Where have you found advice texts?

d Explain the difference between instructions and advice in your own words.

Tip

Think about the first time you used certain resources. You might have needed to refer to guidance texts at that point.

Read the text opposite, which is a guide to stargazing from The Countryside Charity website. Try to identify where the writer is giving instructions and where she is giving advice.

An astronomer's guide to stargazing with the naked eye

by Mary McIntyre

There are few things more mesmerising than sitting outside underneath a dark, starry sky.

You may think that you need a telescope to be a stargazer, but that's not true. There are lots
5 of amazing things you can see with nothing but your eyes, such as **constellations**, planets, the Milky Way, meteor showers, **zodiacal** light or even the aurora borealis (northern lights).

1. Keep comfortable and warm

10 It sounds obvious, but if you are straining your neck and back to look up or if you get cold, you won't be comfortable outside for very long. Lie on a sun lounger where your neck and back are supported. Even in the summer months it can
15 get cold at night, so dress warmly and take a blanket and hot drink out with you.

2. Be aware of the Moon phase

The Moon is gorgeous but it's also a huge source of light so it's not your friend if you're
20 stargazing. You can check the Moon phases and rise and set times for your location on the Time and Date website or using a smartphone app such as Lunescope. Plan your stargazing session for a time when the Moon is out of
25 the way.

3. Plan your observing goals beforehand

Some constellations or targets are seasonal and are therefore only visible at certain times of the year so make sure you've done your
30 research before heading out. You can use the free Stellarium app, star chart or **planisphere**.

Milky Way

From the UK, the Milky Way is best observed from late spring to early autumn when the
35 whole arch is higher and the colourful region closer to the galactic core is visible. The galactic core is the centre of the Milky Way.

Meteors

Sporadic meteors (shooting stars) can occur
40 at any time but there are several principal meteor showers that occur every year, such as the Perseids in August or the Geminids in December, when you may see many more meteors per hour. The exact date of a meteor
45 shower peak changes from year to year.

Zodiacal light

The zodiacal light is a faint cone of light caused by sunlight scattering off **interplanetary dust**. It is best observed from a dark sky location,
50 during spring (in the west after sunset) or during autumn (in the east before dawn).

Aurora borealis (northern lights)

Aurora is only visible from the UK when there is a **geomagnetic storm** but at certain
55 parts of the **solar cycle** this happens quite frequently, especially in the northern half of the UK. Download a good aurora notification app such as Glendale to alert you when this may be possible. It will usually be quite low in the
60 northern sky and will not look as colourful as photographs suggest.

---

constellation – group of stars forming a pattern

zodiacal – linked to the zodiac, a belt-shaped region of stars in the sky

planisphere – a star chart made up of two disks that shows which stars can be seen and when

interplanetary dust – small particles floating in outer space between planets

geomagnetic storm – (also known as a 'magnetic storm') a short disturbance of the Earth's magnetic field and atmosphere

solar cycle – repeated changes in the sun over an 11-year period

⭐ Boosting your vocabulary

Skilled writers chose their words with care. The activity below explores some of the vocabulary used in the source text, which has been highlighted on page 89.

Activity 2

a The writer says that few things are 'more mesmerising than sitting outside underneath a dark, starry sky'. The adjective 'mesmerising' means holding someone's attention completely so they cannot be distracted.

The words below have a similar meaning to 'mesmerising'. Which do you think is closest to 'mesmerising' in meaning and why?

gripping   fascinating   spellbinding   captivating

entrancing   interesting   enthralling

> **❓ Did you know?**
>
> The verb 'to mesmerise' comes from the name of an Austrian doctor, Franz Mesmer, who used a therapy technique on his patients, which was later developed into hypnotism.

b The writer refers to 'sporadic meteors', then goes on to compare them with important meteor showers that happen every year. The word 'sporadic' comes from a Greek word *sporas* meaning sown or scattered in a random way.

  i Think of a synonym for 'sporadic' and use it in a sentence of your own.

  ii Think of an antonym for 'sporadic' and use it in a sentence of your own.

> **🔑 Key term**
>
> **homophone** a word that sounds the same as another, but is spelled differently and means something different

c The adjective 'principal' means the most important, main or chief. It is often confused with the noun 'principle' which means a truth or rule that influences behaviour or reasoning. The two words are **homophones**, which means they sound the same but are spelled differently.

Read the sentences below and decide which ones use the words correctly.

I was given the principal role in the school play.

As a matter of principal, I am a vegan.

Her behaviour suggests that she has absolutely no principles.

The principle sat on stage, in front of other members of staff.

💡 Building your knowledge

Instruction texts

The purpose of instructions are to tell people what to do. Instructions need to be clear for the reader, so they should be short, direct and concise, to avoid any **ambiguity** or confusion.

You can generally recognise instructions because they contain the features below.

- They are listed with numbers, letters or bullet points.
- They usually start with an imperative (command), such as 'take', 'look', 'find', 'put' or 'go'.
- Instructions use the **second person** to directly address the reader, so they may use the pronoun 'you' and the **possessive determiner** 'your'.

Activity 3

a Identify some of these features in the source text on page 89.

   i Write down the three *main* instructions.

   ii Underline the imperatives.

   iii Circle the feature that shows they are part of a list.

   iv Highlight any pronouns or determiners that directly address the reader.

b Why do you think instruction texts use these features?

c Write another instruction to add to the list for stargazing. Remember to keep it short and direct and start it with an imperative. Your instruction might be about where to go stargazing, who to go with or your own idea.

If you look at the presentation and structure of the text, you will notice that the three main instructions stand out because they are printed in bold. Under each instruction there is a short paragraph giving more details and reasons for the instruction. The tone in these paragraphs is more informal and they use more **colloquial language**. For example, the writer describes light from the moon as very strong and says 'it's not your friend', meaning it will not help your stargazing.

🔑 Key terms

ambiguity having more than one meaning

colloquial language informal words or phrases that are suitable for ordinary conversation, rather than formal speech or writing

possessive determiner a word that comes before a noun to show whose it is, e.g. *my, your, her*

second person addressing the reader directly, using the pronoun 'you'

Advice texts

In the second part of the stargazing guide, the writer gives advice to readers on where, when and how to see the most dramatic, impressive astronomical features in the night sky.

As with most advice texts, the writer isn't telling the reader what they *must* do, but making suggestions as to what they *could* do and giving reasons for these suggestions. An advice text is less commanding than an instruction text and tends to be more detailed, often containing factual information.

In advice texts, writers often make suggestions using **modal verbs** or adverbs. For example, the writer uses an adverb to suggest that the Milky Way 'is best observed' from late spring to early autumn. She goes on to explain why (when the arch is higher and more easily seen). The final sentence is a statement giving more factual information.

> **🔑 Key term**
>
> **modal verb** a verb that works with another verb to show that something needs to happen or might possibly happen, e.g. *must, shall, will, should, would, can, could, may* and *might*

Activity 4

a   The text includes detail about the three astronomical features in the table below: meteors, zodiacal light and aurora borealis.

  i   Identify an example that makes suggestions about these features, using modal verbs such as 'may' or adverbs such as 'usually' or 'best', and add it to the second column of the table.

  ii   Identify an example that includes factual information and add it to the third column of the table.

Astronomical feature	Suggestion	Factual information
Meteors	You 'may see' more meteor showers per hour in August or December.	The Perseids occur in August; the Geminids in December. The exact dates change each year.
Zodiacal light		
Aurora borealis		

b   Look at the examples in your completed table. How would the text differ if it only included factual information?

c   What is the effect of the writer using modal verbs and adverbs to suggest advice for the reader? Choose the most suitable answer below.

  •   The reader knows that there are many choices available.

  •   The reader can use the writer's expert knowledge to make good choices.

  •   The reader is being told exactly what to do.

d   Summarise the differences between instruction texts and advice texts. Think about the purpose of each and how a writer chooses to present each in terms of structure and language features.

Activity 5

Write another short section of advice for the stargazing guide. Use the heading 'The best stargazing places in the United Kingdom'. Use the fact file opposite to help you with information.

Fact file - The best UK locations for stargazing

Features:
- quiet, large, open spaces
- small population
- very little 'light pollution' (artificial sources of light, such as streetlights)

Wales is a world leader in protecting its land for night skies. Some of the best areas in Wales for stargazing are:
- Snowdonia National Park
- Elan Valley
- Brecon Beacons

Putting it all together

Activity 6

Now you are going to write your own guide text, using the skills you have learned and practised in this unit. It should be instructional and offer advice. Follow the steps below.

Step 1: Decide on the topic of your guide text (for example, advice on a new hobby, sport or visiting a new place). Think carefully about the purpose and audience of the text and consider what that means for the tone of your writing.

Step 2: Plan your guide with a careful structure. Remember, you will need to include a title, introduction and a combination of advice text and instructions.
Instructions:
- are short and clear
- start with an imperative
- are listed with numbers or bullets
- directly address the reader as 'you'.

Advice texts:
- are written in longer sentences
- include modal verbs and adverbs to give suggestions
- include factual information to guide readers.

Step 3: Write your guide using the ideas in your plan from Steps 1 and 2. Finally, refer back to your earlier ideas and decide how successful you have been.

2.6 How do writers provide explanation?

In this unit, you will:

- learn about explanation texts and their conventions

- explore the effects of structure and language features in an explanation text

- comment on how a writer uses the features of an explanation text in an article.

What's the big idea?

The long-term consequences of technology and AI (artificial intelligence) are often debated. Some people fear that increasing dependence on robotics (machines that assist humans) is dangerous, as they may spiral out of control or become cleverer than humans. Other people believe that technology is vital to help humans survive on planet Earth.

In this unit, you will look at an article focusing on how the wonders of technology can be used to help save the environment. In particular, you will explore how the writer explains the benefits of driverless cars in an engaging, informative way for readers.

⚙ Activity 1

Look at the two images of robots on this page.

a   What are the similarities and differences between the images? What do they suggest about the qualities and characteristics of futuristic technology?

b   What stories or films do you know about robotics or AI? Do they stir up wonder or terror in you, or other emotions?

⚙ Activity 2

The article you are going to read in this unit is an explanation text. Think of other explanation texts you have read in this chapter. What sort of features do you expect to see?

The article below is from an organisation called Greener Ideal and explains how driverless cars will have a positive effect on the environment. As you read, think about how the writer engages the reader with a careful choice of language and tone.

The Environmental Benefits of Driverless Cars

by Ashleigh Rose-Harman

By now it's clear that a future with mostly (if not all) driverless cars on our roads is a matter of *when*, not *if*.

There are many **societal** and environmental implications that make a driverless future exciting for environmentalists. This article takes a look at some of the positive developments a driverless future will bring. But first, let's look at exactly what a driverless car is.

What is a driverless car?

Driverless cars, also referred to as self-driving cars or **autonomous** cars, are vehicles that don't require a person to manually control them. You don't need to have your hands on a steering wheel, and in some cases, there isn't even a steering wheel to hold. […] In general, a driverless car's computer system takes over all driving responsibilities. The vehicle's system uses infrared radars, LIDAR (laser radar), as well as sophisticated motion sensors, cameras, incredibly accurate GPS, and complex algorithms that allow the car to drive itself.

Using all of this technology, along with historical data from logged hours, the car can generate a map of its surroundings to know where it's going, what's around it and what areas to avoid. The car can read road lights, traffic signs, road markings and even monitor other vehicles, cyclists and pedestrians. The car drives by the rules of the roads, meaning speed limits are always adhered to and obstacles and potential hazards are spotted much quicker allowing for a safer halt, with less braking and accelerating.

Emissions

Yes, most of the driverless vehicles being driven (and test-driven) today are already fully electric. But even so, unless your car's battery charge is powered entirely by clean energy, you're still indirectly contributing to **emissions** (though, not nearly as much as a gas engine). Autonomous cars use significantly less gas and energy when driving, compared to a vehicle driven by a human.

Most gas is burned when driving at high speeds, braking, and re-accelerating excessively. Self-driving vehicles cut these factors out of their driving style, meaning less gas is burned, or battery power consumed, resulting in less air pollution. […]

Traffic congestion

In addition to emissions and city **smog**, traffic **congestion** in general is an inconvenience for most city dwellers. Valuable urban areas are reserved for highways and thoroughfares, in many cases leaving little to no area for pedestrians, cyclist or parks.

Congested city streets and highways will be a distant memory when all of the vehicles on the road are driverless. [Researchers have developed a new traffic light system for driverless cars that will allow traffic to move] more steadily, opening up new opportunities for city planning that focuses on pedestrians and green space rather than traffic flows. […]

In conclusion

Driverless cars are undoubtedly a boon for the planet. Not only will they help curb emissions […] and allow city planners to focus on green space more than roads, they'll also give every commuter more time in their days.

---

societal – linked to society
autonomous – having the freedom to control itself
emissions – things that are given out during a process, such as poisonous fumes

smog – air pollution (originally a mix of 'smoke' and 'fog')
congestion – over-crowding

⭐ **Boosting your vocabulary**

Skilled writers choose their words with care. The activity below explores some of the vocabulary used in the source text, which has been highlighted on page 95.

Activity 3

a The noun 'implications' means the likely consequences of something. For example:

> There are many positive implications of riding a bicycle, such as getting fitter and not needing as many lifts from your parents.

Write a sentence using this noun to show you understand its meaning.

b The word 'manually' means by hand. It comes from the Latin word *manus*, meaning hand.

How do you think the following words link to the idea of hands?

manipulate   manicure   manuscript

c The word 'monitor' can have different meanings. It can be a noun or a verb. Read the meanings below and decide which is the most appropriate in the context of the article.

- A student who is given special duties in a school.
- A screen used in a studio to check and control transmissions.
- To record information about how things are working.

d The word 'adhere' comes from the prefix ad- and a Latin verb *haerere*, meaning 'to stick'. Write two sentences using the verb 'adhere'. The first sentence should use the literal meaning of something physically sticking to something else. The second should use the figurative meaning of follow closely, support or believe in.

❓ Did you know?

The word 'explain' is linked to the Latin word *planus* which means plain or clear. An explanation is a statement or an account that makes something clear to the reader or listener.

💡 Building your knowledge

The purpose of an explanation text is to explain something to the reader, increasing their knowledge and understanding about how something works, an event or a process. An explanation text may also explain how something might provide a solution to a problem. In the extract, the writer is considering how driverless cars can be part of the solution to the issue of environmental pollution.

A well-crafted explanation text is clearly structured. Explanation texts often include the following structural features:

- a heading
- an introductory paragraph
- subheadings
- a concluding paragraph.

This helps to achieve the purpose and enables the reader to follow the explanation clearly.

> ✅ **Tip**
>
> Think about how the reader is addressed, the vocabulary choices, the enthusiasm of the writer.

Activity 4

a Find examples of the structural features listed above in the explanation text on page 95.

b What is the purpose of these structural features? Match each feature to one of the functions below.

To explain the purpose of the article	To briefly tell the reader what the article is about
To sum up the key points of the explanation	To divide up the information for the reader

c **i** Briefly summarise the positive reasons for using driverless cars.

   ii How were you able to find the information for your summary? Think about how the structural features helped you to find the information you needed.

   iii Why are structural features important in an explanation text?

Explanation texts usually include the following language features:

- technical language to provide more information about the process being explained, e.g. 'emissions', 'infrared radars'
- statements that contain facts, e.g. 'Most gas is burned when driving at high speeds'
- sentences written in the present tense to describe the process, e.g. 'Autonomous cars use significantly less gas and energy when driving, compared to a vehicle driven by a human.'
- **multi-clause sentences**, e.g. 'Self-driving vehicles cut these factors out of their driving style, meaning less gas is burned, or battery power consumed, resulting in less air pollution.'

Key terms

clause a part of a sentence with its own verb

multi-clause sentence a sentence with more than one clause, each with its own main verb, e.g. *The judge frowned and lifted her hammer.*

Activity 5

a Find more examples of the features listed above in the article on page 95. Note them in a table like the one started below.

b Think about the effect of each feature and explain its impact on the reader.

Feature	Evidence	Effect it creates for the reader
Technical language	'GPS, and complex algorithms'	Increases the reader's knowledge
Facts		

Stretch yourself

Rewrite lines 16–22 without using any technical vocabulary. How does this change the impact of the explanation?

Putting it all together

Activity 6

You have explored the structure and language features of an explanation text. Now you are going to put together all you have learned by writing a response to the question below.

> How does the writer use structure and language features to explain the benefits of driverless cars?

You may find it helpful to follow the structure and some of the sentence starters below, or you can use your own.

> Introduction: The purpose of the text is to explain how… to an audience of people interested in…

> The article opens with a focus on… The language is interesting because the writer makes use of… (insert feature) … (insert evidence) in order to explain/highlight/develop the idea of/engage…

> Next, the article progresses to include…

> Then, the writer builds the explanation by…

> Finally, the writer concludes the explanation by…

Read the example of how one point is explored below:

> The writer uses technical language in the article, referring to details such as 'GPS, and complex algorithms'. The effect of including technical language is that it increases the reader's knowledge of the subject and gives credibility to the writer's expertise, making it seem a reliable, authoritative resource.'

✅ Tips

- Remember to plan your essay first. Try to analyse at least one language feature in each paragraph.
- When you talk about features, remember to explain how they help the meaning of the text, appeal to the intended audience and contribute to the text overall.

2.7 How do we compare texts?

In this unit, you will:

- learn how to structure a comparison of two texts
- explore how a writer's choice of language and register is shaped by purpose, audience and context
- compare two texts written on a similar topic.

What's the big idea?

The development of new science and technology can create mixed responses. Many people are full of wonder and excitement, but others fear that changes may bring difficult, even frightening consequences.

In this unit, you will look at two non-fiction texts about the development of new technology – robots and AI. The first writer is full of wonder and excitement; the second writer explains ways of controlling and safeguarding AI in the workplace. The two writers use very different language, structure and tone, reflecting the different purposes and audiences the texts were written for.

This unit will help you to develop your skills when comparing texts, learning how to:

- pick out key ideas
- summarise information
- structure your comparison
- use suitable language to connect your ideas.

⚙ Activity 1

a List three words or phrases that could be used to help you compare things, for example different books, films or places. There is an example below to help you.

> Although I like…, I prefer…

b What do you find challenging when comparing texts? You might agree or disagree with the students' opinions below or note down something else in your own words.

There's too much information to think about.

I don't know what sort of things to compare.

I'm not sure how to structure a comparison.

I don't know what sort of words and phrases to use.

The text below is an extract from a newspaper article written in 1958. The article is about the development of a new robot, which has some human characteristics.

Text A

Meet the one-eyed robot – it's fantastic

by Nicholas Lloyd

A FANTASTIC one-eyed robot is being built that may be taught to recognise its master. It will welcome the master with a mechanical grunt, and it will read, write, see, hear, learn.

Dr Wilfred Taylor, 33-year-old lecturer in **anatomy**, hopes to finish the £34,000 robot at London University by 1960.

It will be more intelligent in some ways than a small child. Its 4000 electronic 'nerve cells' will work like a human brain.

Perfected

Dr Taylor has already perfected one robot with 40 cells, which learned five letters of the alphabet. The new one will learn the whole alphabet – and numbers, too. In theory, this amazing technical feat could be developed to produce a brain capable of absorbing a complete adult education. The problem is that the average man packs 100 million cells inside his skull, and Dr Taylor needs a fair-sized room to house his 4000 artificial ones.

anatomy – the study of the structure of living things

Activity 2

a What does the word 'master' in line 2 suggest about the relationship between the robot and its owner?

b The writer uses the adjective 'fantastic' twice. What other adjective does he use to express his sense of wonder?

c What skills does the writer expect the robot to achieve in the second sentence? What is the effect of presenting them in a list?

d What facts does the writer add to impress the reader about the robot's brain?

The second extract is from a website, MIT News. The article was written in 2023 to inform companies about a new platform, Verta, that helps to control AI in the workplace.

Text B

Helping companies deploy AI models more responsibly

by Zach Winn

Verta offers tools to help companies introduce, monitor, and manage machine-learning models safely and at scale.

Companies today are incorporating artificial intelligence into every corner of their business. The trend is expected to continue until
5 machine-learning models are incorporated into most of the products and services we interact with every day.

As those models become a bigger part of our lives, ensuring their integrity becomes more important. That's the mission of Verta, a startup that spun out of MIT's Computer Science and Artificial
10 Intelligence Laboratory (CSAIL).

Verta's platform helps companies deploy, **monitor**, and manage machine-learning models safely and **at scale**. Data scientists and engineers can use Verta's tools to track different versions of models, audit them for **bias**, test them before deployment, and monitor their
15 performance in the real world.

"Everything we do is to enable more products to be built with AI, and to do that safely," Verta founder and CEO Manasi Vartak says.

monitor – watch, record and test
at scale – in large quantities or sizes
bias – inaccurate information

? Did you know?

MIT (Massachusetts Institute of Technology) is a prestigious American university, world famous for its role in the development of modern technology and science.

Activity 3

a   AI is playing a bigger part in our lives and work. What words and phrases does the writer use to emphasise this?

b   How would you describe the tone of this text? Choose two adjectives from the list below or think of your own. Explain your choices.

fun   precise   enthusiastic   businesslike

serious   professional

c   In the final paragraph, Vartak sums up the purpose of Verta. Rewrite what she says in your own words.

Stretch yourself

Read the statements below. Which ones do you agree or disagree with and why?

- 'Robots are wonderful and offer exciting opportunities for society.'
- 'Robots are taking over and AI means they will soon be smarter than us. It's terrifying.'
- 'Robots can fail and then what will happen? We rely on technology too much.'

⭐ Boosting your vocabulary

Skilled writers chose their words with care. The activity below explores some of the vocabulary used in Text B on page 102, which has been highlighted.

Activity 4

a   If one thing 'incorporates' another thing, it includes it. Write a sentence using the word 'incorporate'.

b   If you have 'integrity' as a person, you are honest, trustworthy and clear in your beliefs. What do you think this word means if it describes a machine-learning model (AI)?

c   The word 'audit' means to examine officially. What other technical language can you identify in the text?

💡 Building your knowledge

When you compare texts, you need to think about similarities and differences. You should consider not just *what* is said, but also *how* it is said. Below are some of the different aspects you should focus on in a comparison.

Topic: This is the subject matter of the text, i.e. what it is about. Some texts can have the same general topic but differ in the detail.

Activity 5

a   The two texts in this unit are about the same general topic. What is it?

b   What different aspect of that topic does each text focus on?

Context: This is understanding when and where texts were written, and how this influenced the writers.

Activity 6

a   When were each of the source texts written?

b   How does this affect each writer's point of view about the topic?

Purpose: This is the reason the texts are written.

Activity 7

What do you think is the main purpose of each text? Choose one or two purposes from the list below and give reasons for your choices.

to entertain   to inform   to explain

to instruct   to advise   to persuade

Audience: This is the people that the writer expects to read the text. For example, they may be children or young people, academics, the general public, business people, voters or consumers (buyers).

Activity 8

a Who do you think is the intended audience for each text?

b Use a quotation from each text to help explain your answer.

Language: The language of a text includes the vocabulary it uses, the tone that it creates and the **register**. The register is linked to the style of the writing, whether it is informal, neutral or formal. Informal language is the sort of language we use in conversations, including commonly used words and phrases, emotional expressions and personal opinion. Formal language tends to be more complex, uses specialist vocabulary and contains less personal expression.

🔑 **Key term**

register the manner of speaking or writing, which can range between formal and informal

Activity 9

a How would you describe the register of each text in this unit? Choose from the options below and give reasons for your answer.

informal   neutral   formal

b Look back at some of the language features explored in Unit 6. Which features do these two writers use in their texts? How do these features influence the tone and register of these texts?

When you are comparing texts, you will need to use comparative vocabulary to link your ideas and point out differences and similarities.

Activity 10

Sort the words and phrases opposite into those that show differences and those that show similarities.

whereas   both   in contrast   in the same way

neither   on the other hand   unlike   similarly

Putting it all together

Activity 11

Use the skills and knowledge you have gained in this unit to answer this question:

Compare how the writers of the two texts present their ideas about AI technology.

In your answer you should consider: topic, purpose, audience, language and context. You may find it helpful to plan your answer by noting key points in a table like the one started below.

Things to consider	Text A	Text B
Topic	The development of the one-eyed robot	The development of Verta to check AI systems
Purpose	To inform and entertain	
Audience		

Remember to use comparative vocabulary to highlight the differences and similarities, linking your ideas together. You may find some of the following sentences helpful in structuring your response.

The texts were written in different contexts and at different times. We can tell this because…

The language used in Text A is… In contrast, the language in Text B is…

The language shows that the texts are aimed at different audiences. For example…

Overall, the texts show that the writers have different perspectives on and attitudes towards the development of robots and AI. The writer of Text A is excited, whereas the writer of Text B is… The reasons for this could be…

2.8 How do writers present themselves?

In this unit, you will:

- learn how an autobiography can inform and entertain a reader

- explore the conventions of autobiographies, such as the use of chronological order, the past tense, facts, opinions and description

- write an extract from your own autobiography about something you have done.

What's the big idea?

In the last three units, you have read a variety of non-fiction texts inspired by the wonder of space and scientific and technological developments. In this unit, you will discover how one person's autobiography can give readers a wonderful insight into a remarkable career. The writer is Katherine Johnson, whose work at the American space agency NASA helped to send the first American astronauts into space and ultimately on to the Moon.

In this unit, you will also explore the language and structural conventions of an autobiography extract and develop skills to write a short extract from your own autobiography.

⚙ Activity 1

a   Name two people that you admire and have read about.

b   Where did you learn about them, for example in a **biography**, an **autobiography**, online or in a book?

c   What sort of features would you expect to find in an autobiography?

🔑 Key terms

autobiography the story of a person's life, written by that person

biography the story of a person's life, written by someone else

In her autobiography, Katherine Johnson explains how, as a gifted mathematician, she worked with NASA scientists and engineers on complex calculations, before computers were introduced.

In this extract, Johnson talks about the recruitment of America's first astronauts and her work on a space research project, Project Mercury, along with her colleagues.

Extract from *My Remarkable Journey: A Memoir* by Katherine Johnson

1 The remaining seven astronauts were introduced at a press conference in April 1959, and they became instant celebrities. They were the walking embodiment of our nation's space dreams. They were willing to risk their lives to travel to the unknown and push the boundaries of human exploration. [...]

2 It had been decided from the start that a rocket booster would fire the **ballistic capsule** into space, like a bullet shot from a gun. For the initial **suborbital flight**, the capsule would go up into space, turn, and head right back down for a landing in the Atlantic Ocean. US Navy ships would be on standby to pull the capsule and our first space explorer out of the water and back to safety. Project Mercury's ultimate goal, though, was to orbit the Earth, and that **trajectory** – a circular path around the planet – was far more complex. Ted knew more than practically anyone at **Langley** about how to figure out the trajectory for this. So he was tasked to write the report that would lay out the path of NASA's first orbital flight. I wanted in on it, too.

3 "Let me do it," I suggested to Ted. "Tell me where you want the man to land, and I'll tell you where to send him up."

4 He didn't hesitate to let me run with it. We collaborated on the report, but much of the math was my work. So when Ted and Carl left our division to join John in the Space Task Group [another team], Ted suggested to our boss, Mr Pearson, that I should complete the report. Mr Pearson wasn't the most progressive fellow when it came to women in the workplace, but he agreed to let Ted move on and for me to finish what we had started.

5 Just after Thanksgiving in 1959, I handed over the thirty-four-page report, full of all kinds of equations, a couple of launch case studies, tables with sample calculations, lots of charts, and reference texts. [...] The report went through the agency's usual detailed process of review, analysis, and revisions before publication in September 1960.

6 I was extremely proud of the work Ted and I had put into the research and even prouder that our work would be used to direct NASA's first flights into space. So I had signed my new [married] name – Katherine G. Johnson – to the report, just like the men. It was a rather assertive move at the time because women just didn't do that, even though they often contributed significantly to the work. When the report was published, it was the first time a woman of any race in my division had been listed on the research paper as a co-author.

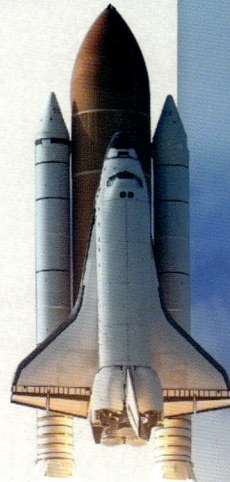

---

ballistic capsule – the part of a spacecraft that carries the instruments or crew
suborbital flight – the flight of a spacecraft into space and its return, without orbiting (going round) the planet from which it was launched
trajectory – pathway
Langley – NASA's oldest research centre

⭐ Boosting your vocabulary

Skilled writers choose their words with care. The activity below explores some of the vocabulary used in the source text, which has been highlighted on page 107.

Activity 2

a The word 'embodiment' means someone or something that represents an idea or feeling. In the text, Johnson describes the astronauts as the 'embodiment of our nation's space dreams'. This means they physically represented the hope that the nation had of successfully going to space. Write two sentences of your own that include the word 'embodiment'.

b To 'collaborate' means to work together. The prefix 'co-' means jointly, or together with. Which of the words below use the prefix 'co-' meaning together? Explain the meaning of the words you have chosen.

coastline   cooperate   coalesce   coconut   coincidence   collate

c Complete a Frayer model to show your understanding of the word 'assertive', like the one started below.

Frayer model

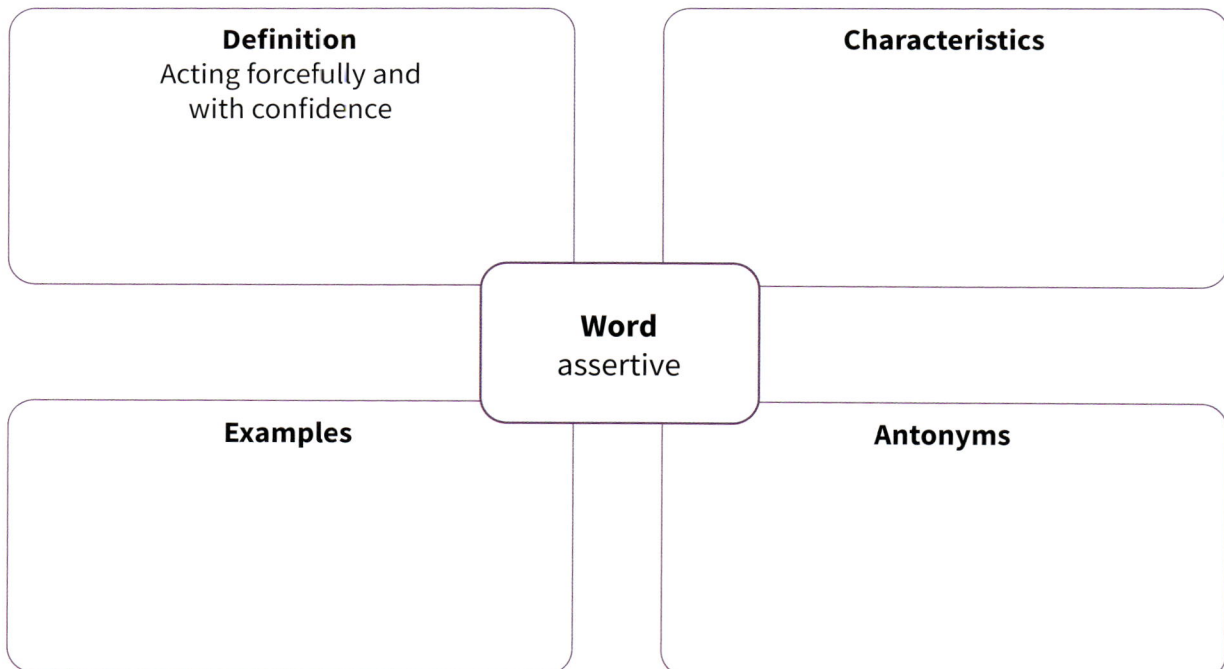

Definition	Characteristics
Acting forcefully and with confidence	

Word
assertive

Examples	Antonyms

💡 Building your knowledge

An autobiography is a type of **recount**, which means that the writer is telling the reader about what has happened in the past. So, most of recounts are written in the **past tense** and as a **first-person narrative** (with the pronouns 'I' or 'we').

Activity 3

a   Read the sixth paragraph again. Identify the verbs in the past tense and examples of the first-person pronoun. What effect do these have?

b   If the text had been written in the **third person** (as a biography, rather than an autobiography), how might it change the impact on the reader? For example, 'Katherine was extremely proud of the work she and Ted had put into the research'.

✏️ c   Write a few sentences about one of your first experiences, for example your first day at a new school or a visit to a new place. Remember to use the past tense and first-person pronouns.

Another feature of autobiographies is that events tend to be told in **chronological order**. This means that the order of events in the text follows a steady timeline from the past towards the present.

🔑 Key terms

chronological order the order in which things happened

first-person narrative a story told by someone as if they were involved in the events themselves, using first-person pronouns, e.g. *I* and *we*

past tense a verb form that shows actions or events that have already happened

recount an account (written or spoken) of an event or experience

third person a narrative voice that informs the reader of what is taking place, using the pronouns *he*, *she* or *they*

Activity 4

a   Number the events below from 1 to 6 to show the order in which they occur in the text. Number the first event 1.

Publication of report   Press conference

Handing over the report   Ted and Carl moved to the Space Task Group

Ted was asked to write the report   Katherine offered to help on the report

b   In the sixth paragraph, Johnson talks about a significant event in the history of female research in her division (department). Explain it in your own words.

Most autobiographies include facts. These help to fulfil the purpose of the text to inform the reader, giving them context for understanding the writer's experiences. They also usually include the writer's opinions and feelings. Remember, facts can be proven to be true; opinions and feelings will vary from person to person.

Activity 5

a   Write down one fact given in paragraph 1 of the extract and two facts given in paragraph 2.

b   What opinion does Johnson express in paragraph 4?

c   What feeling does Johnson describe in paragraph 6?

d   How does this mix of fact, opinion and feeling help to convey the writer's voice and personality to the reader?

> **? Did you know?**
>
> Katherine Johnson was one of the first African American women to work as a NASA scientist. The story of her work was told in the 2016 film *Hidden Figures*.

A good autobiography will entertain the reader, as well as give them facts and information. This entertainment may come partly from the style of writing, including humour or powerful description. Johnson uses emotive language to show how exciting the prospect of travelling into space was at the time. She also uses imagery to create vivid pictures in the reader's mind.

Activity 6

a   What words and phrases does Johnson use in paragraph 1 to stir up emotion in the reader? (Think about how astronauts were regarded and the hopes they embodied.)

b   What simile does Johnson use in paragraph 2, and how does it emphasise the power and speed of the ballistic capsule travelling through space?

c   Write a sentence using a simile to help describe something that you did or witnessed recently. For example:

> The students stood like statues, too scared to move as the Head strode towards the shattered glass.

⬆ Stretch yourself

Johnson uses a mix of specialist technical vocabulary (such as 'ballistic capsule' and 'suborbital flight') and more colloquial language (such as 'I wanted in on it, too') which has a more personal, conversational tone and register. Discuss the effects of this combination on the reader.

Putting it all together

Activity 7

Write an extract that could be in your own autobiography, which is about something you have done or are proud of. It might be an act of kindness, overcoming a difficulty or achieving something else.

Plan your answer first. Remember to include some of the key conventions, such as:

- writing in the first person, using 'I' and 'we'
- using the past tense (mainly)
- recounting events in chronological order
- facts and information to give context and help the reader's understanding
- opinions and feelings
- entertaining description, for example using powerful imagery and emotive language.

Stretch yourself

Rewrite a section of your autobiography extract with a different tone and register, to achieve a particular effect. For example, you might include some technical specialist vocabulary relating to a sport or craft, along with more conversational language conveying your opinion or feelings.

WILD PLACES AND URBAN LANDSCAPES

When we talk about place, we often think about location: for example, the position of an object in space, an actual place we have visited, an unfamiliar country or even the name of a town on a map. However, when writers talk about place, they do more than just provide us with a location.

A writer's presentation of place helps the reader to understand and appreciate the setting of the text. In addition to the location, setting gives us information about the people in the place and when the story events are set (for example in the past, present, future, or at a specific time of the day). The description of a setting will also reveal a writer's attitude towards the place, linking to themes and ideas they want to share, as well as communicating a mood or atmosphere to the reader.

Settings can be real or imaginary. In this chapter, you will explore non-fiction and fictional settings. Some of these settings may be familiar, others may transport you to unfamiliar and exciting locations.

⚙ Use what you know

a   Think about your favourite places. These can be local places or ones further away that are familiar to you. Why do you like them?

b   What books have you read that contain memorable places? Why were they memorable?

c   Why do you think it is important to learn about different places and how writers feel about them?

d   Look at the places shown in the images numbered 1-6 on these pages. Discuss how you feel about these places. What assumptions do you think we make about these places?

Words you need to know

landscape, urban, rural, marginal, futuristic, environment, climate fiction, coast, nature, wasteland

3 Learning overview

This learning overview will show you where the chapter will take you on your learning journey. Use it to help you plan your learning, monitor what you have learned and then evaluate your knowledge.

3.1 How are attitudes towards place conveyed?
116–121

Prepare
- What are the different attractions of city life and rural living?

What I will learn
- How writers convey their attitudes to place.
- How to compare texts.

How I will learn
- Read two extracts and consider the different perspectives.
- Compare the presentation of place by two different writers.

3.2 How are new places presented in literature?
122–127

Prepare
- Why can unfamiliar places be both exciting and unsettling?

What I will learn
- How writers create a strong narrative voice.
- How dialect contributes to a sense of character and place.

How I will learn
- Explore the narrative voice in a novel.
- Write a description of an unfamiliar place using a distinctive narrative voice.

3.3 How do poets present the power of nature?
128–133

Prepare
- What do you already know about Romantic poetry?

What I will learn
- How a poem is structured for effect.
- How a poet conveys mood.

How I will learn
- Read a sonnet and identify themes and ideas.
- Write a commentary about the mood and message of the poem.

3.4 How is setting used to create tension?
134–139

Prepare
- What can make a familiar place appear threatening?

What I will learn
- How a writer uses the senses to describe setting.
- How a writer uses language and structure in interesting ways.

How I will learn
- Explore narrative tension in a story opening.
- Write the opening of a story, disrupting reader expectations.

3.5 How do writers make ordinary places interesting?
140–145

Prepare
- Do urban areas consist only of bricks, steel and glass?

What I will learn
- What is meant by 'marginal land'.
- How writers juxtapose urban and rural imagery.

How I will learn
- Read an extract to explore the writer's use of language and structure.
- Write about the author's attitude towards marginal places.

3.6 How are shifting landscapes presented?
146–151

Prepare
- What do you know about how the landscape changes?

What I will learn
- How writers create a specific mood.
- How texts can borrow the characteristics of another genre.

How I will learn
- Read an extract and identify language choices.
- Describe a place using contrasting moods.

3.7 How can we write about environmental issues?
152–157

Prepare
- What do you know about persuasive devices?

What I will learn
- The features of classical rhetoric.
- How writers structure an argument.

How I will learn
- Read an article and identify its structural features.
- Write and present a speech about an environmental issue.

3.8 How do writers describe future spaces?
158–163

Prepare
- What do you know about science fiction?

What I will learn
- The features of climate fiction.
- How writers create dystopian places.

How I will learn
- Read an extract and identify themes and images.
- Evaluate a text's success in conveying a future world.

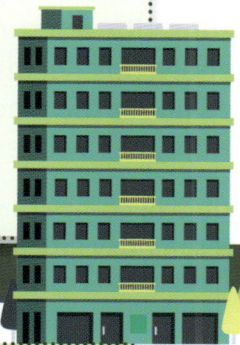

3.1 How are attitudes towards place conveyed?

In this unit, you will:

- learn how writers reveal attitudes towards place
- explore what is meant by a writer's tone
- compare how two writers convey attitudes towards place.

What's the big idea?

When writers describe a setting (real or imaginary), they may show it as friendly, hostile, magical or just quite ordinary. They may be excited about the place or they may be disappointed. The language they use will reveal these emotions.

In this unit, you will compare writers' attitudes towards two very different places: a busy city and an area of quiet countryside.

⚙ Activity 1

a Think of a description of a place that you found powerful or exciting. It could be from fiction or non-fiction. What made it memorable for you?

b Think about other fiction you have read. Why is the **setting** important?

The first text in this unit is a letter written in 1801 by Charles Lamb to his friend, the poet William Wordsworth. Wordsworth had invited Lamb to spend time with him in the Lake District. However, in his letter, Lamb explains to Wordsworth why he would much rather stay in London.

Trafalgar Square in 1898, a famous public square in London

Derwent Water in the Lake District

Activity 2

a Look at the two paintings opposite. Both date from around the time that Lamb was writing. Choose words from below to describe each painting.

bustling   exciting   overwhelming   splendid

beautiful   rich   colourful   tranquil

majestic   peaceful   chaotic   dangerous

b Based on these images, why do you think Lamb might prefer to stay in the city rather than visit the mountains and lakes? You could use some of the words above to help you write your answer.

Key terms

setting where the action takes place

tone the writer's (or speaker's) feeling or attitude expressed towards their subject

As you read the letter below, think about Lamb's attitude towards London (his viewpoint) and the **tone** he uses to convey his feelings.

Extract from a letter from Charles Lamb to William Wordsworth, 1801

Separate from the pleasure of your company, I don't much care if I never see a mountain in my life. I have passed all my days in London, until I have formed as many and intense local attachments as any of you mountaineers can have done with dead nature. The lighted shops of the **Strand** and **Fleet Street**; the
5 innumerable trades, tradesmen, and customers; coaches, wagons, playhouses; all the bustle and wickedness round about **Covent Garden**; [...] the **watchmen**, drunken scenes, **rattles**; life awake, if you awake, at all hours of the night; the impossibility of being dull in Fleet Street; the crowds, the very dirt and mud, the sun shining upon houses and pavements; the print-shops, the old-book stalls [...]
10 coffee-houses, steams of soups from kitchens; the pantomimes, London itself a pantomime and a masquerade – all these things work themselves into my mind, and feed me without a power of satiating me. The wonder of these sights impels me into night-walks about her crowded streets, and I often shed tears in the **motley** Strand from fulness of joy at so much life. All these emotions must be
15 strange to you; so are your **rural** emotions to me.

Strand, Fleet Street, Covent Garden – places in London
watchmen – people who patrolled the streets to reassure people and check on property

rattles – noisy conversations
motley – varied and diverse
rural – to do with the countryside

117

⭐ Boosting your vocabulary

Skilled writers choose their words with care. The activity below explores some of the vocabulary used in the source text, which has been highlighted on page 117.

Activity 3

a   The word 'satiating' is another word for 'satisfying'. Both words come from the Latin **root** *satis* meaning 'enough' or 'full'. Think carefully about the meaning of the words below. Which word does not derive from the root *satis*?

> insatiable   satin   satisfactory   saturated

b   'Masquerade' refers to a costumed event in the text. It is also another word for a disguise or mask. It is taken from the Italian word *maschera*, which looks like the word 'mascara'. What is 'mascara'? Explain why the word 'mascara' might come from *maschera*.

🔑 Key terms

figurative language words or phrases with a meaning that is different from the literal meaning

narrator a person who tells a story, especially in a book, play or film

root the core of a word that has meaning. It may or may not be a complete word

💡 Building your knowledge

The tone of a text is the attitude or feelings the author chooses to convey through their choice of language and structural features, e.g. an angry tone, a reflective tone, an excited tone. When exploring the tone of a text, you should think about:

- the *details* that the writer focuses on and why they have selected these details
- the writer's *style*: vocabulary, sentence structure, **figurative language** and other language devices
- what the writer wants the reader to *learn, understand, think* and *feel* about the place.

Activity 4

a   What details does Lamb focus on when describing the city? Look at his use of nouns and lists.

b   Why do you think Lamb focuses on these details?

c   Lamb refers to London as 'a pantomime and a masquerade'. What literary device does Lamb use here and what effect does it create?

d   How do you think Lamb feels about 19th-century London? Find a quotation from the letter to support your answer.

Stretch yourself

How do you think Wordsworth may have responded to this letter? Write a short reply, thinking carefully about the tone.

The second text in this unit was written by Sara Maitland while she was living in Weardale in the north of England. In this extract, the **narrator** describes a summer morning in the hills and moorland.

Extract from *A Book of Silence* by Sara Maitland

At sunrise, as at sunset, particularly in the summer months, the wind often drops, so that even in very exposed places there can be a period of great calm, especially if the weather is clear. I became attentive to those early mornings, which came so gradually. The stars would fade and the black sky turn indigo.
5 The distance emerged, colourless out of the darkness. The sky would change colour: indigo, grey, cream. The view opened out and away mysteriously. The horizon line like a shadow separated the sky from the **moor.** The sky would go on changing: grey, cream, peach. Although the sun rose to my left in the east, because of the **conformation** of the hills, the first sight of it was to my right; the
10 western hills would catch fire first, the sunshine suddenly falling on them in a splash of brightness. The sky would still be changing: cream, peach, white, palest blue. On the moor there were very few songbirds, so this extraordinary silence was not broken by that joyful but insistent clamour, but occasionally there would be **buzzards**, hunting high, floating against the enormous blue. Sometimes the
15 rising sun would catch them from below and the moth-markings of their under-wings would light up suddenly, tawny gold as they rode the bright air. On some lucky mornings there was an extra bonus: overnight the valley would have filled with a thick mist, which did not rise as high as the cottage, or as the moor the far side of the **dale**, so I could contemplate the glory of this making of the day, as
20 though above and outside the world, looking out over a shimmering lake of mist, barely stirring in the dawn calm.

---

moor – an open area of hilly land covered mainly with grass and heather

conformation – shape

buzzards – large, common birds of prey in Britain

dale – a valley (especially in northern England)

Activity 5

In this activity, you will consider the writer's tone and their attitude towards the place they describe.

a   Maitland focuses on several features in her description. Rank the following in terms of their importance to her and explain your decision.

the sky   the hills and valleys   the buildings   the wildlife

b   Maitland's description is full of movement. Find examples of movement and explain what effect you think the writer is trying to create. For example:

Quotation	Effect
'The distance emerged'	It is as if the sky is like a veil that has dropped and she can now see the landscape.

c   What is the writer's attitude towards the scene she is describing? Choose a sentence or two from the text and explain what feelings these express.

   i   Decide how you will plan and write a successful answer to the question above. Look at the example below to help you.

'the western hills would catch fire first, the sunshine suddenly falling on them in a splash of brightness.'

The writer's attitude is one of awe and wonder. The use of the phrase 'catch fire' suggests that the light from the sunrise creates an explosion of light and colour, as if the hills have been ignited. Furthermore, the noun 'splash' suggests that the light appears in an instant, as if it is thrown out by the sun.

The opening sentence presents the 'big idea'.

This phrase shows an understanding of a writer at work.

This comment links the phrase to its literal meaning, 'ignited', and a figurative interpretation of 'an explosion'.

Comments on this noun further develop the big idea.

   ii   Write your answer considering what you have learned from the above.

Putting it all together

Activity 6

In this final activity, you are going to compare the writers' attitudes to the places in both texts, looking in particular at the similarities and differences in their tone.

Step 1: Begin by planning the points of your answer. Choose *two* words below to describe the tone of each text. You could choose two contrasting words if you want to highlight the differences in their tone or two related words to show how the texts are similar in tone.

contemplative   admiring   joyful   intense   passionate   critical

sarcastic   arrogant   excited   cheerful   dismissive

Step 2: For each of the words you have chosen, select a quotation to support your choice and then explain the reason for your choice. For example:

Lamb – critical tone	
Quotation	**Explanation**
'I don't much care if I never see a mountain in my life'	This shows that he dislikes the countryside and much prefers city life.

Step 3: Make a list of connectives and comparative adjectives that you will use to link your points.

Step 4: Using your notes from the steps above, write a response to the following question:

Compare Lamb's and Maitland's attitudes to the places they describe.
You could comment on:
- the details they focus on
- the tone they use.

You may find the writing frames below helpful when presenting similarities and differences between the two texts.

Lamb feels… about the city. This is shown by the word/phrase… which suggests that…
Similarly,/On the other hand, Maitland's tone is… This is shown by the word/phrase…
which suggests that…

3.2 How are new places presented in literature?

In this unit, you will:

- learn how writers use narrative voice to describe unfamiliar places

- consider how language choices and narrative voice create character and place

- write a short description of an unfamiliar place using a distinctive narrative voice.

What's the big idea?

In the last unit, you looked at non-fiction texts and how writers convey their feelings about the places in which they live. In this unit, you will look at an extract from a work of fiction and read a description of a place from the perspective of a narrator who feels like an outsider. You will also explore how the writer uses an interesting – and unconventional – narrative style to create a strong narrative voice.

⚙ Activity 1

a What is the strangest place you have read about in a story? Explain why it was strange and how the writer made it appear that way.

b Have you ever found yourself in an unfamiliar place, for example a new school or new home? How did you feel at the time? Write a sentence to describe how this felt.

🔑 Key term

dialect a form of a language linked to a specific region, e.g. Geordie in Newcastle upon Tyne

After the Second World War, many people from Caribbean countries came to Britain to live and work. Although they did many of the jobs needed to help rebuild Britain's post-war economy, early migrants (people moving to a new country to find work or a better life) faced racial discrimination, exploitation and financial hardship.

❓ Did you know?

People who migrated from Caribbean countries to the United Kingdom between 1948 and 1971 are known as the 'Windrush generation', named after one of the first ships that brought people from Jamaica to London.

Sam Selvon's novel *The Lonely Londoners*, written in 1956, captures the sense of dislocation felt by those early migrants. In this extract, the narrator describes Galahad's first encounter with the city of London. Selvon's novel is written in a **dialect**.

Extract from *The Lonely Londoners* by Sam Selvon

Galahad make for the **tube** station when he left **Moses**, and he stand up there on **Queensway** watching everybody going about their business, and a feeling of loneliness and

5 fright come on him all of a sudden. He forget all the brave words he was talking to Moses, and he realise that here he is, in London, and he ain't have money or work or place to sleep or any friend or anything, and he standing

10 up here by the tube station watching people, and everybody look so busy he frighten to ask questions from any of them. You think any of them bothering with what going on in his mind? Or in anybody else mind but

15 their own? He see a **test** come and take a newspaper and put down the money on a box – nobody there to watch the fellar and yet he put the money down. What sort of thing is that? Galahad wonder, they not afraid

20 somebody thief the money?

He bounce up against a woman coming out of the station but she pass him like a full **trolley** before he could say sorry. Everybody doing something or going somewhere, is only

25 he who walking stupid.

On top of that, is one of those winter mornings when a kind of fog hovering around. The sun shining, but Galahad never see the sun look like how it looking now. No heat from it, it just

30 there in the sky like a force-ripe orange. When he look up, the colour of the sky so desolate it make him more frighten. It have a kind of **melancholy** aspect about the morning that making him shiver. He have a feeling is about

35 seven o'clock in the evening: when he look at a clock on top a building he see is only half-past ten in the morning. [...]

Suddenly Galahad feel a hand on his shoulder and though he want to look and see who it is, is

40 as if the hand paralyse him and he can't move. He just stand there and he hear a voice say: 'Move along now, don't block the pavement.' When he was able to look Galahad see a policeman near him. Again, he panic, though

45 he ain't do anything against the law. Still is so people in **Trinidad** when police near them, as if, even though they ain't commit a crime, the policeman would find something wrong that they do and want to lock them up.

---

tube – the underground railway network in London

Moses – Galahad's friend

Queensway – a shopping street in west London

test – a person

trolley – a bus powered by overhead cables (like a tram)

melancholy – sad

Trinidad – an island in the Caribbean

⭐ Boosting your vocabulary

Skilled writers choose their words with care. The activity below explores some of the vocabulary used in the source text, which has been highlighted on page 123.

Activity 2

a   The word 'desolate' comes from the Latin *de* meaning 'thoroughly' and *solus* meaning 'alone'. It can describe a place but can also describe a person's mood.

Here are some **synonyms** for 'desolate':

| abandoned | bereft | bleak | devastated | dismal | miserable | wretched |

Use three of these synonyms in two separate sentences, first to describe a place, then to describe a person's feelings.

b   The word 'aspect' in this extract refers to a particular appearance or look. The Latin root, *spect*, means 'look'. What other words in English use this root and are connected to 'looking'?

💡 Building your knowledge

Writers often adopt a particular style to create a strong **narrative voice** for the narrator in their story. In his novel, Selvon uses a Caribbean English dialect, instead of **Standard English** (formal language) to capture the character of his narrator. This makes the account sound much more realistic.

Read the facts about dialect below.

Dialects contain different words, grammar and **pronunciation** from Standard English. They can be written and spoken.

Dialects of English vary from region to region. They contribute to a speaker's sense of identity and belonging to a place.

Familiar objects will have different words for them depending upon the dialect. For example, an alleyway in Leeds might be called a 'ginnel' and in Sussex it's a 'twitten', while in the Black Country it might be called a 'gulley'.

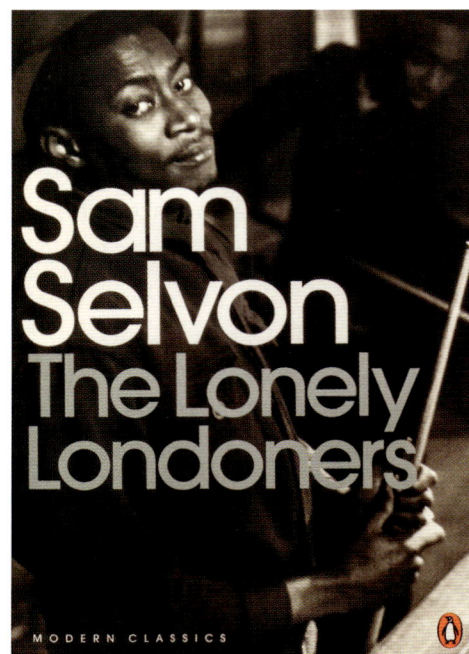

Sam Selvon
The Lonely Londoners

MODERN CLASSICS

Look carefully at the grammatical features of the dialect used in *The Lonely Londoners* and how it differs from Standard English.

Dialect in *The Lonely Londoners*	Quotation	Standard English
Consistent use of the **present tense**, often missing out the main verb 'to be' ('is')	'he standing up here by the tube station'	He *is standing* up here by the tube station.
Leaving out **pronouns** (particularly 'it')	'is one of those winter mornings'	*It is* one of those winter mornings.
Mixing singular and plural forms	'He bounce up against a woman'	He *bounces* up against a woman.

Key terms

narrative voice the perspective (viewpoint) from which a story is told, and the style in which it is told

present tense a verb form that describes actions which are happening now

pronoun a word used instead of a noun or noun phrase, e.g. *he, it, they*

pronunciation the sound made when a word is spoken

Standard English a widely recognised, formal version of English, not linked to any region, but used in schools, exams, official publications and in public announcements

synonym a word or phrase that means the same, or almost the same, as another word or phrase

Activity 3

a   Write a definition and provide an example of both Standard English and dialect in your own words.

b   Match each of the following quotations from the text to the dialect features listed in the table above.

i
'Everybody doing something or going somewhere'

ii
'Suddenly Galahad feel a hand on his shoulder'

iii
'He have a feeling is about seven o'clock in the evening'

c   Selvon uses Standard English for the police officer's speech. What is the effect of this? Read the following statements and decide which one you agree with the most. Explain your decision.

It gives the police officer authority.

It provides a clear separation between the narrator and the police officer.

It helps Selvon build a more convincing sense of place and character.

125

Selvon once said: 'I experimented with the language as it is used by Caribbean people. I found a chord, it was like music.' This suggests that there were pleasing patterns of sound and structure in the dialect of Caribbean English.

Selvon made the decision to use this dialect In his novel to reinforce how out of place the character Galahad feels in his new and unfamiliar surroundings.

Activity 4

a   Why do you think Selvon wrote *The Lonely Londoners*? Think about:
   • Selvon's background
   • the **context** of when Selvon was writing the novel.
   Look back at page 122 to help you.

b   How does Selvon use the Caribbean dialect to help him to achieve his purpose?

Selvon uses many language techniques to create the 'music' of Galahad's narrative voice, including:
• long **complex sentences** with lots of **clauses**
• **repetition** of words and phrases
• a variety of sentence forms, such as **rhetorical questions**.

Activity 5

a   Find examples in the extract of each of the above features.

b   How do these techniques help us to understand Galahad's character and the fact that he is in an unfamiliar place? Think about what these techniques might suggest about Galahad's sense of uncertainty.

c   Write another sentence or two to continue the story. Try to include some of the features listed above. You could describe some of the people at the station, the different buildings, or even the trains.

🔑 Key terms

clause a part of a sentence with its own verb

colloquial language informal words or phrases that are suitable for ordinary conversation, rather than formal speech or writing

complex sentence a multi-clause sentence with at least one subordinate clause, e.g. *He stopped because he was tired.*

context the time, place and influences on a text from when it was written, and from when it is read, which shape our understanding of the text

repetition using the same word or phrase more than once

rhetorical question a question asked for dramatic effect and not intended to get an answer

Putting it all together

In this unit, you have looked at how writers describe place and create narrative voice.

Activity 6

a What techniques have you learned about in Selvon's writing that you could apply to your own writing?

b Write a description of a person who has found themselves in a brand new place for the very first time. They are a little bit afraid of what they see and confused at all the new things.

Try using some of the techniques you have learned about in this unit to capture the 'voice' of your narrator. Here is one student example, with some annotations to help you craft your own work.

> I race through the dark gulley overgrown with weeds, my breath spilling out of me in cold rags. I am alone here and I want to get home. This place is alien to me and every shadow is a threat, every tree a hiding place for some demon waiting for me as I pass by. Why did I get off the bus at the wrong stop? Why didn't I just call home? Borrow the money for a taxi? At the end of the gulley, a shadow. I was doomed. A voice calling out from the blackness. "'Ere, where you goin'? Why you runnin'?" A friendly voice. My breathing slowed…

- Present tense adds immediacy
- Repetition emphasises isolation
- Rhetorical questions build the character's growing frustration
- Short and grammatically incomplete sentences have dramatic impact
- **Colloquial language** captures speaker's authenticity

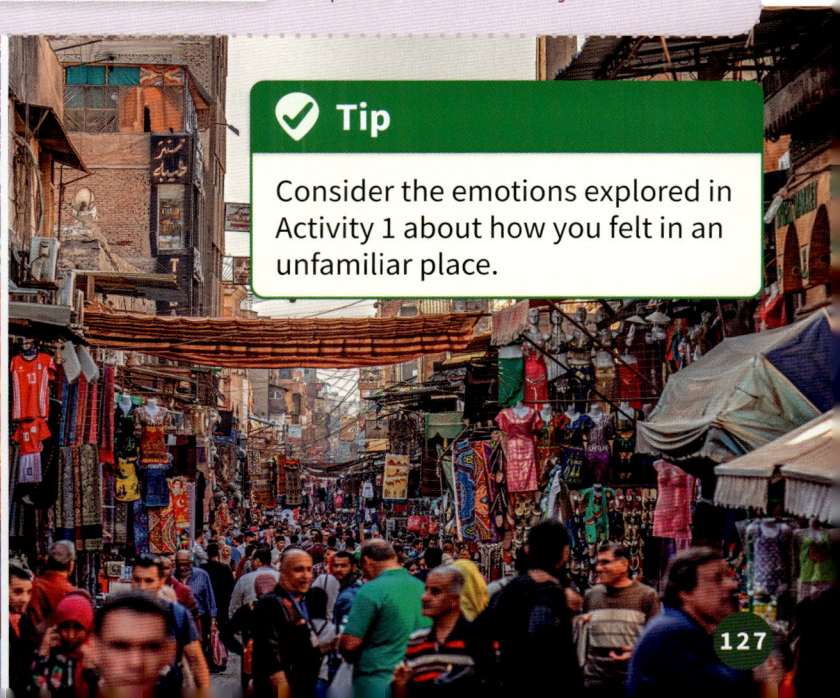

Tip

Consider the emotions explored in Activity 1 about how you felt in an unfamiliar place.

127

3.3 How do poets present the power of nature?

In this unit, you will:

- learn how a poet conveys the power of a natural landscape
- explore how poetic structure and imagery are used to create mood
- analyse a poem for what it reveals about the poet's attitude to nature.

What's the big idea?

In the last two units, you looked at examples of prose, both fiction and non-fiction, and considered how writers use tone and voice to describe urban and rural places. In this unit, you will develop your understanding of structure, mood and attitude by looking at a poem written in the late 18th century. Like the prose texts we have studied, it expresses the writer's strong feelings about a place.

Activity 1

a   Make a list of the poems and poetic techniques that you already know of.

b   The poem in this unit describes the experience of being on the beach at night. What other books, poems or films do you know that use the beach as a setting?

c   Imagine standing on a shoreline. What might you see, hear or feel?

d   Look at this photograph. Choose three of the words below that best describe the scene and explain your choices with reference to details in the image.

eerie   isolated   ominous   unsettling   peaceful   awe-inspiring

This **sonnet** was first published in 1798 in Charlotte Smith's novel *The Young Philosopher*. It was given the title 'Written near a port on a dark evening'.

Smith was notably a poet of the **Romantic era** and, like other Romantic poets such as William Wordsworth, Mary Robinson, William Blake and Lord Byron, Smith presents nature as both awesome and intimidating.

'Written near a port on a dark evening' by Charlotte Smith

Huge **vapours** brood above the **clifted** shore,

Night o'er the ocean settles, dark and mute,

Save where is heard the **repercussive** roar

Of drowsy **billows**, on the rugged foot

5 Of rocks remote; or still more distant tone

Of seamen, in the anchored bark, that tell

The watch relieved; or one deep voice alone,

Singing the hour, and bidding "strike the bell."

All is black shadow, but the **lucid** line

10 Marked by the light surf on the level sand,

Or where afar, the ship-lights faintly shine

Like wandering **fairy fires**, that oft on land

Mislead the **pilgrim**; such the **dubious** ray

That wavering reason lends, in life's long darkling way.

---

vapours – sea-mist
clifted – split, broken
repercussive – echoing
billows – large waves
lucid – bright

fairy fires – light caused by gas from decaying plants, often seen over water and associated with supernatural spirits
pilgrim – a traveller, usually who journeys to a holy place
dubious – doubtful, uncertain

Key terms

prose written language in its ordinary form, rather than poetry or drama

Romantic era a cultural movement in the late 18th and early 19th centuries, which emphasised intense emotion and idealised the natural world

sonnet a short poetic form, typically of 14 lines with ten syllables per line

Did you know?

The Romantic poet Samuel Taylor Coleridge once said that **prose** is 'words in the best order', while poetry is 'the best words in the best order'. Consider your view on this statement after completing this unit.

Tip

As well as focusing on the natural world, this poem also includes gothic elements, which you may recognise from your work in Chapter 2.

⭐ Boosting your vocabulary

Skilled writers choose their words with care. The activity below explores some of the vocabulary used in the source text, which has been highlighted on page 129.

Activity 2

a Smith uses words that are now **archaic**. Look at the archaic words below and match them to their modern meaning. The first one has been done for you.

Archaic words	Modern meanings
bark	often
bidding	boat
afar	in the distance
oft	increasingly dark
darkling	telling or commanding

(bark is matched to boat)

b The poet describes reason as 'wavering', which suggests that it is unsteady and changes direction rather than following a direct path. How does this image link to the idea of someone waving, or a wave on the seashore?

🔑 Key terms

archaic old-fashioned, from a different historical time

iambic pentameter a line of poetry with five iambic 'feet'. An iambic foot is a pair of syllables: one unstressed syllable followed by a stressed one (as in 'da DUM')

quatrain a stanza of four lines, often with a strict rhythm and rhyme scheme

rhyming couplet two consecutive lines of poetry that have rhyming final words

💡 Building your knowledge

Smith's poem is a sonnet. Here are some facts about its form and structure.

- The sonnet has 14 lines and is written using the repetitive beat of **iambic pentameter**.
- The sonnet form is traditionally used for romantic love poems.
- Sonnets are tightly structured. This one consists of three **quatrains** followed by a **rhyming couplet**. Each of the quatrains has a strict rhyming scheme (ABAB).
- The first two quatrains focus on a particular subject or theme. The third quatrain shifts the focus slightly.
- In the final couplet, the poet reflects on the important ideas that the scene or object of the poem represents.

Activity 3

In this activity, you are going to consider the structure of the poem.

a Read the sonnet again. Match each section with what the author is focusing on at that point in the poem.

Sections

Focuses

Lines 1–4

The poet describes the sea mists rising above the cliffs, the coming of the night and the sound of the waves on the shore.

Lines 5–8

In this section, the poet draws attention to the images of light but also suggests that light can be deceptive.

Lines 9–12

In this section, the poet considers what the scene represents and suggests that, like the lights out at sea, life does not always deliver what it promises.

Lines 13–14

The poet shifts her focus to the distant sounds of the sailors out at sea and hears their conversation as they swap their guard duties.

b Find a suitable quotation from the poem to support each of your decisions.

c Why do you think Smith chose to write her poem in the form of a sonnet? Think about what sonnets were traditionally used for and the era this one was written in.

The poem is full of contrasting **imagery**, for example the contrast of silence and noise in 'dark and mute' and 'repercussive roar'. Smith presents nature as both intimidating and powerful but also quiet and tranquil. Smith also uses the structure of the sonnet to show these mixed feelings, as the focus and mood shifts throughout.

> 🔑 **Key term**
>
> **imagery** language that creates pictures in the reader's mind

Activity 4

a Write a definition of the word 'contrast' and list one synonym and one antonym.

b Find other examples of where Smith uses the following contrasts:

  i light and dark

  ii height and depth.

c Why do you think Smith uses these contrasting images?

Smith uses language to create a powerful mood in the poem. For example, she uses **personification** to describe the way the sea-mists ('vapours') hang over the shore:

> Huge vapours brood above the clifted shore,

🔑 Key term

personification showing something non-human as having human characteristics

Smith's use of personification in the poem helps to convey her feelings about the incredible power of nature: she describes the natural world as though it has a mind of its own.

The word 'brood' means to think deeply and constantly about something that is worrying us. Smith makes it sound like the mists are deep in anxious, silent thought, like a person.

Activity 5

a Find other examples of personification in the poem. For each example, explain what effect you think the writer is trying to create.

b What is the overall mood of the poem? Follow the steps below to write a response.

> **Step 1:** Choose one of the words below and explain how it describes the mood of the poem.
>
> isolation   terrifying   tranquil   intimidating   overwhelming   intense
>
> **Step 2:** Use a quotation to support your point.
>
> **Step 3:** Develop your response by adding a comment on what the quotation suggests about the relationship between the poet and the world she describes.
>
> For example:

I think the mood of the poem is one of isolation. ← Statement of mood

This is shown by the reference to the 'more distant ← Quotation
tone of seamen'. The adjective 'distant' suggests

that the poet's position on the shore separates ← Explanation
her from life at sea. It is almost as if the sailors
and the poet are cut off from each other. This

reinforces the theme of loneliness in the poem and ← Further development
could symbolise how the poet feels that we are all
in danger of living in isolation from each other.

Putting it all together

Activity 6

Read the statement and question below.

'The mood is really miserable and the poet has nothing positive to say about nature.' To what extent do you agree with this statement?

Write your response to this question. You could refer to the following:

- how the structure of the poem highlights particular parts of the landscape
- Smith's use of language to evoke the power of nature
- the poem's overall message.

Here are some sentence starters you might use:

Although the poem is brooding, I think that there are also some moments of light…

I agree that the poem offers very little hope. Even though Smith describes some examples of light, there are…

Stretch yourself

William Wordsworth said that English poetry owes a lot to Charlotte Smith but it is unlikely she will be remembered. Why do you think Smith is often overlooked when people talk about the Romantic poets?

3.4 How is setting used to create tension?

In this unit, you will:

- learn how writers use setting to create narrative tension

- explore how narrative perspective, foreshadowing and sensory description help to build tension

- write the opening of a story, using descriptions of the setting to build tension.

What's the big idea?

In this unit, you will read an extract from a contemporary novel and explore how the writer presents a place familiar to her that is both reassuring and threatening. As in previous units, you will look at attitudes towards place and the writer's use of language and structure to build tension through use of setting. You will also think about how the writer disrupts the reader's expectations and creates narrative tension.

🔑 Key term

tension a feeling of being on edge with nerves stretched tight

⚙ Activity 1

a How do writers create **tension**?

b Read the quotations below, which have been taken from the opening page of the novel *An Emotion of Great Delight*.

'a brief, fragrant breeze'   'I released the breath'   'I was stone'

'Airplanes droned overhead'   'It felt good'

'sweaty hands that braced my face'   'I was going nowhere'

'Cars rushed by'   'It was a perfect summer day'

i What type of place do you think is being described here?

ii What mood is created by these quotations?

iii What do you think this text is going to be about?

The novel, *An Emotion of Great Delight*, tells the story of Shadi, a Muslim American teenager, and is set at the time of the 9/11 terrorist attacks and the subsequent invasion of Iraq. The extract opposite is from the opening to the novel.

Extract from *An Emotion of Great Delight* by Tahereh Mafi

The sunlight was heavy today, fingers of heat forming sweaty hands that braced my face, dared me to flinch. I was stone, still as I stared up into the eye of an unblinking sun [...] I loved it, loved the blistering heat, loved the way it seared my lips.

It felt good to be touched.

It was a perfect summer day out of place in the **fall**, the stagnant heat disturbed only by a brief, fragrant breeze I couldn't source. A dog barked; I pitied it. Airplanes droned overhead, and I envied them. Cars rushed by and I heard only their engines, filthy metal bodies leaving their excrement behind and yet—

Deep, I took a deep breath and held it, the smell of diesel in my lungs, on my tongue. It tasted like memory, of movement. Of a promise to go somewhere, I released the breath, anywhere.

I, I was going nowhere.

There was nothing to smile about and still I smiled, the tremble in my lips an almost certain indication of oncoming hysteria [...] I laid backward on dusty **asphalt**, so hot it stuck to my skin.

When I opened my eyes again a ten-thousand-foot-tall police officer was looming over me. Babble on his walkie-talkie. Heavy boots, a metallic swish of something as he adjusted his weight.

I blinked and backed up, crab-like, and evolved from legless snake to upright human, startled and confused.

"This yours?" he said, holding up a dingy, pale blue backpack.

"Yes," I said, reaching for it. "Yeah."

He dropped the bag as I touched it, and the weight of it nearly toppled me forward. I'd ditched the bloated carcass for a reason. Among other things, it contained four massive textbooks, three binders, three notebooks, and two worn paperbacks I still had to read for English. The after-school pickup was near a patch of grass I too-optimistically frequented, too often hoping someone in my family would remember I existed and spare me the walk home. Today, no such luck. I'd abandoned the bag and the grass for the empty **parking lot**.

Static on the walkie-talkie. More voices, garbled.

I looked up.

Up, up a **cloven chin** and thin lips, nose and sparse lashes, flashes of bright blue eyes. The officer wore a hat. I could not see his hair.

"Got a call," he said, still peering at me. "You go to school here?" A crow swooped low and cawed, minding my business.

"Yeah," I said. My heart had begun to race. "Yes."

He tilted his head at me. "What were you doing on the ground?"

"What?"

"Were you praying or something?"

My racing heart began to slow. Sink. [...] I knew anger, but fear and I were better acquainted.

"No," I said quietly. "I was just lying in the sun."

---

fall – autumn
asphalt – tarmac

parking lot – car park
cloven chin – a chin with a dimple in the middle

135

⭐ Boosting your vocabulary

Skilled writers choose their words with care. The activity below explores some of the vocabulary used in the source text, which has been highlighted on page 135.

Activity 2

a The word 'acquainted' means to know someone or something fairly well. What other word, meaning a person or colleague, does this remind you of?

b The word 'frequented' is the past tense of a verb that means to go somewhere often. 'Frequent' can also be used as an adjective to modify a noun. Write two sentences using the word 'frequent' in these different ways.

❓ Did you know?

Mafi uses only 'said' to describe dialogue. The writer Stephen King believes good authors should only use said, because the story ought to be good enough for a reader to instinctively know how characters are speaking.

💡 Building your knowledge

Many writers establish setting at the beginning of their stories to enable the reader to picture the scene and introduce the characters. However, Mafi decides to start by immersing the reader in her character's thoughts. We don't know the character's name, their location, or any motives for their behaviour. Instead, we experience the world through the character's thoughts and senses.

Mafi uses the **first-person narrative**, which enables the reader to share the narrator's feelings about events and other characters in the story. However, this type of narrative voice can be restrictive because the reader is unable to 'listen in' on what other characters are thinking and therefore know what is happening elsewhere in the story. In a first-person narrative, the reader, like the narrator, experiences events as they unfold, which can create both suspense and surprise.

🔑 Key term

first-person narrative a story told by someone as if they were involved in the events themselves, using first-person pronouns, e.g. *I* and *we*

Activity 3

Re-read lines 1–30 of the extract from *An Emotion of Great Delight*. Notice the quotations that you explored in Activity 1.

a How has your reading of the extract affected your first impressions?

b What do we learn about the narrator from this part of the extract?

c How does Mafi create an unsettling mood in this part of the extract? Think about:
  - how she uses the senses to evoke the character's feelings
  - contrasting images of light and dark, hot and cold, or freedom and confinement.

d How does Mafi make the appearance of the police officer at the end of this extract sound surprising?

Mafi slowly reveals small details about the setting through sensory description; the narrator describes what she can feel: 'dusty asphalt'; hear: 'a dog barked', 'airplane droned'; smell and taste: 'the smell of diesel in my lungs, on my tongue'. Mafi's emphasis on the senses, rather than an explicit description of place, helps to immerse the reader in the character's world.

Activity 4

Descriptions in books can often be dominated by what the narrator sees or hears.

a Write a short paragraph to describe a place, real or imaginary, using only the senses of touch, taste and smell.

b What techniques have you used in your writing?

> ✅ **Tip**
>
> Remember different language and structural devices can be used to convey different moods. Look back to Chapter 2, Unit 2 to remind yourself of these.

In the extract, Mafi conveys a sense of underlying anxiety about Islamophobia by showing Shadi as tense. After the 9/11 terrorist attacks, many American Muslims became victims of Islamophobia. There are accounts of young people feeling particularly isolated and singled out in schools during this time, although prejudice and discrimination can still happen in both this and other scenarios today.

In the extract, the weather is used to convey the tension that Shadi is experiencing. Although the sun is shining, there are hints that the atmosphere is hostile. She describes the sunlight as 'heavy', 'blistering' and 'searing' (scorching) her lips. The sun has an 'unblinking' eye, which suggests the intensity of being constantly watched.

Activity 5

Consider the positive and negative connotations for heat.
Find quotations to support these in the extract.

The narrator also builds tension by dropping hints to the reader that something unpleasant is going to happen. This technique of preparing the reader for future events in the story is called **foreshadowing**.

Activity 6

a   How does the quotation 'sweaty hands that braced my face' in the first sentence foreshadow the events and mood of the whole extract?

b   Why might a parking lot be a suitable setting for this scene and why do you think Mafi waits until line 48 to reveal the setting to readers?

c   On line 55 the focus shifts briefly to a crow that 'swooped low and cawed'. In literature, the crow is quite a complex **symbol**. It can signify death and ill fortune, but it can also represent the spirit world and magic. Why might this be an appropriate image to use in this extract? Think about the idea of foreshadowing above.

d   Make a prediction of what will happen next, based on the idea of foreshadowing.

🔑 Key terms

foreshadowing a technique that gives a hint of something that will develop later

symbol something specific that represents a more general quality or situation

Putting it all together

Mafi uses first-person perspective to restrict the reader's knowledge of the fictional world and builds atmosphere and tension by using techniques such as foreshadowing.

Activity 7

✏️ Write the opening of your own story, creating a sense of place that is both familiar and frightening. Use some of the techniques you have studied, such as:

- first person narrator with a restricted viewpoint
- not revealing the exact setting too soon. Make your reader guess where you are!
- describing setting and events through the senses
- surprising the reader by introducing a character unexpectedly
- using foreshadowing and/or symbols to increase narrative tension.

Use this sample answer with annotations below to help you.

> I closed my eyes, the steady hum of an engine and the babble of voices soothing me to a half-sleep. This was the way I liked to begin my days, both in among the throng of humanity but also apart from it. A bell rang, but it could have been a thousand years away for all I cared. Most people liked to plug themselves into their music, but this was my symphony. The world, its people, the energy of the morning. Someone sat next to me. I could sense their warmth, the scent of damp clothes and hair, the rustle of a bag. I kept my eyes closed, not wanting to make contact.
> The bus moved away.

Immersing the reader into the senses – sound, touch, smell

The bell might be a symbol or the foreshadowing of something ominous!

Sudden introduction of a new character

Delayed revelation that the narrator is on a bus

⬆ Stretch yourself

One critic said: 'Mafi successfully creates an oppressive sense of place that conveys the tensions felt post 9/11.'
To what extent do you agree with this statement?

3.5 How do writers make ordinary places interesting?

In this unit, you will:

- learn how writers actively influence the reader's attitude towards place

- explore how juxtaposition, descriptive detail and language choices build up a sense of place

- comment on how a writer influences your attitude towards a place.

What's the big idea?

In the first half of this chapter, you studied a range of fiction and non-fiction texts by writers with different perspectives and attitudes towards rural or urban places.

In the second half of this chapter, you will consider places that don't seem to fit with either of these categories. These places are referred to as 'marginal' places or as 'edgelands' – the patchy areas of nature and wildlife that sit side by side with the built-up areas of towns and cities. Despite the ordinariness of such places, you will learn how writers describe them in ways that encourage readers to appreciate their beauty.

⚙ Activity 1

ugly   historical   worth exploring

fascinating   intimidating   familiar

dangerous   secretive   strange

a   Look at the image below. Read the words and phrases opposite. Which ones would you associate with this image? Explain your decisions.

b   What types of stories might use this place as a setting?

c   How might you connect this image to the 'big idea' at the start of this unit?

In 1973, Richard Mabey set out to explore the 'unofficial countryside' around London. He wanted to examine how nature adapted to increasing urbanisation (the growth of towns and cities) and how it thrived in wastelands, canal-sides, roadsides and disused factories.

Extract from *The Unofficial Countryside* by Richard Mabey

Two stretches of marginal land stick in my memory. The first was wedged between the Thames and the advancing northern edge of the new South London town of Thamesmead.

5 It was early winter and I had been ferreting round the docks and river edges with a friend, looking for wildfowl that were moving closer to London in the wake of the cleaner water. We had no luck peering through the knotholes in

10 the dock fencing and decided instead to look at Thamesmead. It was a desolate journey. The pre-cast concrete tower blocks had only been up a few years, yet they were already stained with the industrial fumes blown over

15 by the river. We failed to discover a single tree, and the only green to be seen was in the few patches of razored lawn. [...]

We hurried on through the estates, past the muddy chaos where the contractors were

20 digging in for the next instalment of this ugly living factory. It wasn't long before we found ourselves in a rough patch of wasteland that hadn't been visited by the bulldozers. It was a relic of the vast areas of marshland that once

25 stretched along both sides of the Thames to the east of London. No one can have used it or cattle grazed it for generations, for it was blanketed with a dense undergrowth of birch, willow and ancient hawthorn.

30 We disembarked from the car and followed a crumbling metalled road deep into the scrub. The air was almost unbreathable, full of sulphur drifting from the power station directly over the river. Yet there was a sense

35 of anticipation, of imminent life, of stirrings and activity in the bushes. Magpies were working through the more open areas, and greenfinches shuttling in tiny bands between the fruit-laden hawthorns. Once we glimpsed

40 a kestrel, a hunched silhouette on a birch top, easing himself around to glare at every quarter of this jungle. It may have been the fading light, or the grimy air, but he seemed a bird made for this place, a swarthy hawk with a

45 bony, no-nonsense body, and none of the flashy elegance of his country relatives.

---

relic – something that has survived from an earlier time
undergrowth, scrub – areas of dense plants, not looked after
birch, willow, hawthorn – types of tree

sulphur – a chemical released from power plants and vehicles
magpies, greenfinches – types of bird
kestrel, hawk – birds of prey

⭐ Boosting your vocabulary

Skilled writers choose their words with care. The activity below explores some of the vocabulary used in the source text, which has been highlighted on page 141.

Activity 2

a   The verb 'ferreting' is a colloquial term for 'rummaging around', but it is also a **metaphor**. Ferrets like to explore and are very curious, so Mabey borrows the characteristics of a ferret to describe his actions. Here are some other words that borrow from the animal world. Find out what they mean and use each of them in a sentence:

waspish	wolfed	sheepish	fishy	sluggish	gander

b   The word 'imminent' means 'about to happen'. It sometimes gets confused with 'eminent', meaning famous or outstanding. Write separate sentences using the two words correctly.

💡 Building your knowledge

During the time he was writing, Mabey witnessed a rapid increase in new construction projects, which were built on areas rich in wildlife. In this extract, he uses **juxtaposition** and contrasts in the text to shift between descriptions of industrial areas and residential areas to places where wildlife is thriving. Juxtaposition involves putting two or more contrasting ideas near each other in a text to highlight their differences: for example the 'concrete tower blocks' and the contrasting 'dense undergrowth of birch, willow and ancient hawthorn'.

Activity 3

One way of exploring the structure of a text is to consider how a writer shifts the focus from one place to another and to think about the order in which these places are presented.

a   Put the following locations in order of when they appear in Mabey's journey.

The pre-cast concrete tower blocks	Crumbling metalled road	The building site

The docks and river edges	Rough patch of wasteland	The scrub

b Why do you think this structure has been used?

c How do you think the text would be different if the industrial descriptions were all together, followed by the wildlife descriptions all together?

Mabey also uses language to create a powerful sense of place. He uses specific nouns to inform us of the different plants and wildlife that he encounters. He also uses vivid imagery, figurative language and appeals to the senses to convey his admiration of the natural world. One way of developing more detailed analysis is by focusing on the effects of specific words and exploring their connotations.

Activity 4

a Find words and phrases in the text that show:

    i the ugliness of the built environment

    ii the busyness of nature.

b When Mabey comes across a building site for a new housing estate, he describes it as 'this ugly living factory'. What is the effect of describing the housing estate in this way? What does this tell us about Mabey's feelings about the buildings and the people that might live there?

c Mabey describes the landscape as constantly moving and evolving. What can you **infer** from the following quotations? Use the sentence stems to help with your answers.

    i 'the advancing northern edge of the new South London town of Thamesmead'

> *By describing the town as advancing, it makes it seem that…*

    ii 'the muddy chaos where the contractors were digging'

> *The word 'chaos' makes me think that the building site is…*

d Why does Mabey think that the kestrel is 'a bird made for this place'? What characteristics does the kestrel share with the marginal landscape?

🔑 Key terms

infer to work something out from what is seen, said or done, even though it is not stated directly

juxtapose to put words, ideas or images together to show a contrast or relationship between them

metaphor a comparison that says one thing is something else, e.g. *Amy was a rock*

Activity 5

Like all writers, Mabey has made conscious decisions about what details to include in his writing. Thinking about the writer's choices helps us to understand their perspective.

a Take one of the following statements and discuss whether you agree or disagree. Find specific words in the text that show the place is glamorous or presented negatively.

> Mabey is being unfair by presenting the city in a negative way.

> Mabey's description of the natural areas makes them sound glamorous.

b Think about how Mabey describes these different areas. Why do you think he focuses on these parts of the landscape and not others? You could use these sentence stems in your discussion:

> Mabey describes the setting as…
>
> I think Mabey's selection of details suggests that…

Tip

When embedding quotations, make them part of your sentence to make your writing sound more fluent.
For example:

✓

Mabey describes the tower blocks as 'stained with the industrial fumes blown over by the river'.

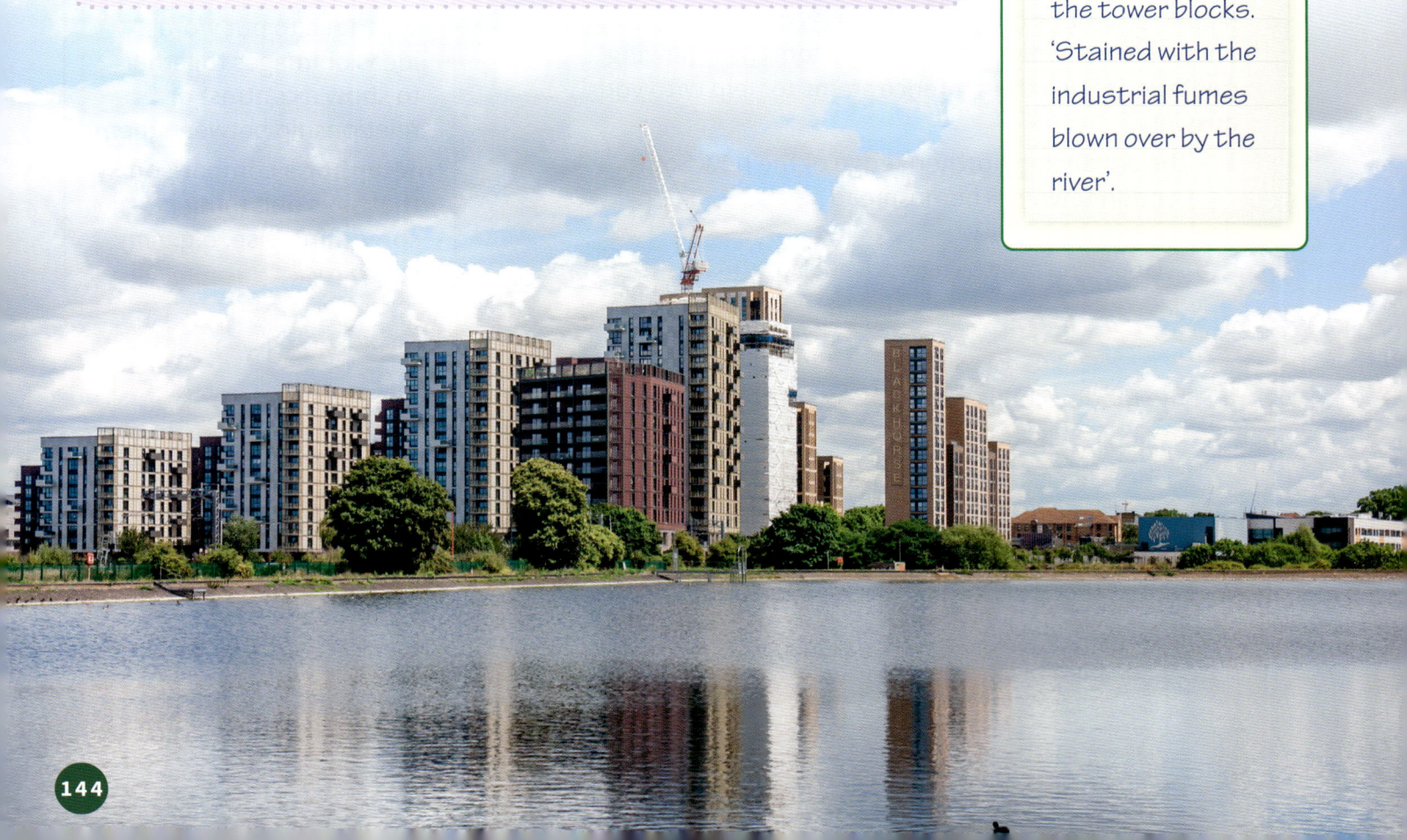

✗

Mabey describes the tower blocks. 'Stained with the industrial fumes blown over by the river'.

Putting it all together

Activity 6

Read the question below.

> 'Mabey emphasises the beauty of nature but also shows how nature and humans can exist comfortably together in these marginal spaces.'
>
> To what extent do you agree with this statement? Think about:
> - the structure of the text
> - the way he describes both the natural and the built environment.

Refer back to work completed earlier in this unit and then follow the steps below to answer this question.

Step 1: Identify to what extent you agree with the statement. Does Mabey show nature is beautiful? Why does he do this? Do you think he shows that humans and nature can live together? What is his attitude towards humans? Think of some synonyms to describe his attitude.

Step 2: Complete the mind maps below to find evidence to support your ideas. Try to match each piece of evidence to the synonyms you have come up with.

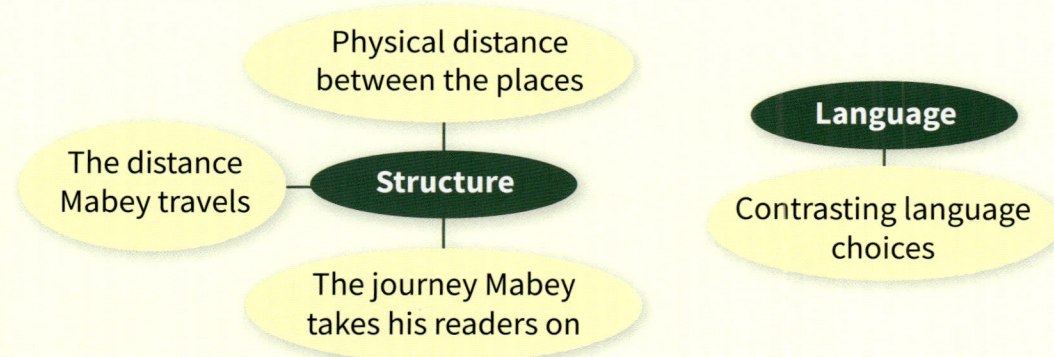

Physical distance between the places

Language

The distance Mabey travels — Structure

Contrasting language choices

The journey Mabey takes his readers on

Step 3: Annotate your evidence with what you think the effect is on the reader. Remember to explore connotations. Look back at Activities 3 and 4 to help you.

Step 4: Write your response, using the planned ideas above. Make sure you:
- make it clear what you think Mabey's attitude to nature is
- use evidence from the text to support your points
- explain how this evidence shows this attitude by exploring connotations and thinking about how it makes the reader feel about the place he is describing.

3.6 How are shifting landscapes presented?

In this unit, you will:

- learn how a writer uses shifting landscapes to create contrasting moods

- explore how writers borrow styles from other genres

- write about a place, creating contrasting moods.

What's the big idea?

In the last unit, you considered how the landscape shifts between the natural world and the built environment.

In this unit, you will learn about how the landscape is not just shifting but disappearing. You will read an account from someone who lives on the edge of an eroding clifftop and how life there is changed by the constantly evolving landscape.

You will also consider the concept of intertextuality, looking in particular at how texts borrow features from different genres (types of story) to convey a variety of moods and effects.

⚙ Activity 1

a   In previous units you have considered the mood of a text. How can you identify the mood of a text?

b   What sort of mood would you expect a writer to create when writing about their experiences of living in a house on the edge of a cliff?

c   What do you think might be the advantages and disadvantages of living on the coast? If you already live in a coastal area, you can draw on your own experiences.

Juliet Blaxland lives in a house on the edge of a cliff on the Suffolk coast. This sounds rather thrilling, and in the following extract from her book, you will discover that the reality is even more dramatic!

Extract from *The Easternmost House* by Juliet Blaxland

We live in a windblown house on the edge of an **eroding** clifftop at the easternmost end of a track which leads only into the sea. The farm track looks as if it wants to continue for a mile or two, but it has been hacked off roughly by the wind and sea and erosion. There used to be a village here, and there used to be
5 several hundred more acres of farmland. [...]

There is much here that 'used to be', and it seems sad and unromantic that the actual easternmost point of Britain is now an uncelebrated spot in Lowestoft. Soon, the house we live in will be described as the house that 'used to be' right on the edge. The jagged edge is always a warning, of recent erosion, of unknown cliff
10 conditions underfoot, of new chunks of land having fallen into the sea overnight.

When we first moved here, there was a house on the edge of the cliff, and about fifty paces to the edge. Now, there are more like twenty paces. We are beginning to adjust our lives and plan for the demolition, before the house is lost to the sea and we must move. [...]

15 The view from the house and the cliff is a distant postcard view of Southwold, but the cliff is a wild place, bashed about by raw nature. In summer it can be like living in a Mediterranean paradise. In winter it can be like living on a wind-lashed **trawler**. The Suffolk coast is eerie and deceptive like that. It looks pretty, but it hides many ways to cast tragedy over the unwary or the over-confident on their
20 summer holidays. [...]

Usually the erosion is gradual and predictable, but sometimes there is a sudden cliff collapse. Two **reedcutters** told me that the Benacre estate, a mile or so to the north, had lost sixteen metres in one tide. Once, a whole **dune** disappeared overnight. In one tidal storm surge, a sandy bay formed on our beach. One night, there was
25 a vast electric storm of horizontal lightning, lighting up the whole barley crop as if in daylight, but with an odd eerie light in the manner of an imagined nuclear explosion. Rarely, the green sky of Northern Lights can be seen from this farm.

One day, quite soon, the yellow digger will destroy the walls where our familiar pictures hang. Then the sea will finally come, and it will devour without gratitude
30 the ancient piece of cliff upon which the house now sits, and this place where we have known a happiness beyond contentment will exist only as only a particular volume of sky over the sea.

---

eroding – being worn away gradually

trawler – a fishing boat

reedcutters – people who harvest reeds, a grass-like plant

dune – a mound of sand shaped by the wind

⭐ Boosting your vocabulary

Skilled writers choose their words with care. The activity below explores some of the vocabulary used in the source text, which has been highlighted on page 147.

Activity 2

a   Complete a Frayer model diagram, like the one below, to explore the meaning and **connotations** of the word 'deceptive'.

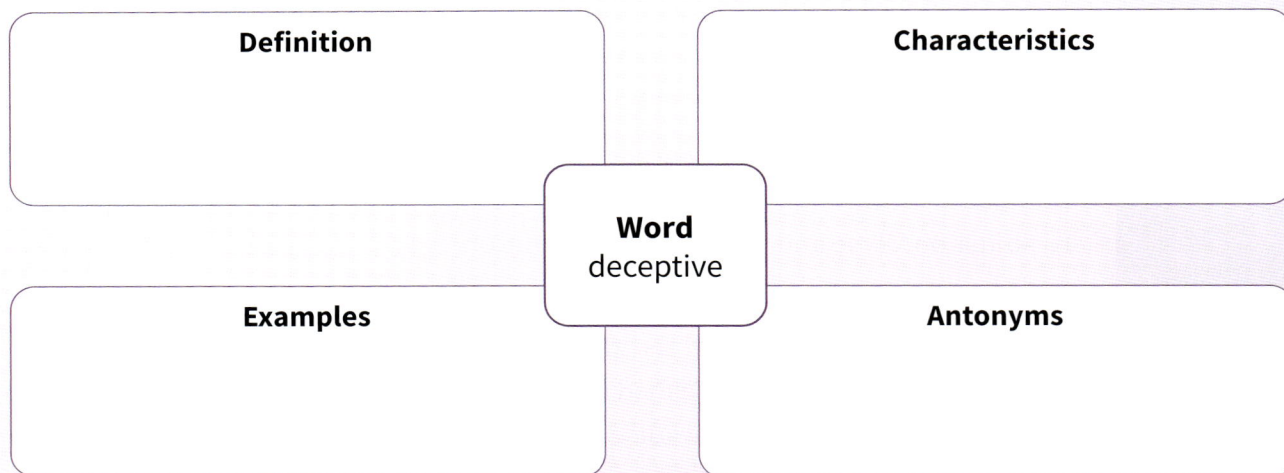

Definition	Characteristics

Word
deceptive

Examples	Antonyms

b   The word 'devour' comes from the Latin word *vorare* meaning to swallow up. It also gives us the word 'voracious', which means having a huge appetite for something. What does this word suggest about the actions of the sea in line 29? Does it sound like a gentle or a violent act?

c   The word 'romantic' has different meanings.
   • It can refer to a sentimental or idealised idea of love between couples: 'They had a romantic candlelit dinner.'
   • It can refer to an idealised attitude to things: 'She had a romantic view of the past.'
   • It can also, as you saw in Unit 3, refer to the Romantic poets (notice the capital 'R').
   What does Blaxland's use of the word 'unromantic' mean?

❓ Did you know?

The area around the Suffolk coast has a reputation for ghostly sightings and other supernatural happenings. As a result, many famous writers, such as M. R. James, have used it as the setting for their stories.

🔑 Key terms

antonym a word that has the opposite meaning of a particular word

connotation an idea or feeling linked to a word, as well as its main meaning

Building your knowledge

The creation of mood is one of the most effective techniques in a writer's toolkit. When we think about mood, we mean the atmosphere and emotional response that the writer wants to create. Mood can be conveyed through narrative structure and the writer's language choices, but it can also be determined by our expectations of a particular type of story or **genre**. For example, we expect ghost stories to create a chilling or unsettling mood, while fantasy and adventure stories will build thrills and excitement.

Key term

genre a type of story, e.g. *horror, romance, adventure, science fiction*

Activity 3

a Write two sentences that create contrasting moods. Try to use the same location. For example:

> The dark grey clouds loomed over the rain-drenched hills. (gloomy mood)
>
> The fluffy clouds drifted slowly over the golden, sun-drenched hills. (joyful mood)

b In the extract, Blaxland paints a rather unsettling image of where she lives, but she also makes it sound attractive. Find a quotation from the text to support each of these interpretations:

  i unsettling   **ii** attractive.

c Which of the words below do you feel best describe the writer's feelings about where she lives? Choose quotations from the text to support your choices.

admiration   regret   concern   anxiety   fear   helplessness

d The mood at the end of the extract is quite sombre. Blaxland fears the loss of not just her home. What else will she lose? Think about the following quotations:

> 'the yellow digger will destroy the walls where our familiar pictures hang'

> 'this place where we have known a happiness beyond contentment'

So far in this book, you have read different types of texts. These types of text can be divided into genres. See the table below for examples.

Type of text	Genres
Non-fiction	travel writing, autobiography, biography
Fiction	romance, gothic, science fiction, fantasy

Each of these genres has particular **conventions** and recognisable styles. For example, in fiction: in a horror story you might expect to encounter spooky castles, thunder and lightning, ghosts and monsters. In non-fiction, travel writing will describe a writer's experiences of a place: it may include facts and opinions about the place.

Activity 4

Choose one genre from the table above and discuss what conventions you would expect it to include.

Some texts might borrow the conventions of other genres. For example, you might come across elements of the romance genre, such as a love story, in a detective novel. This is a form of **intertextuality** (linking between individual texts). The extract from Blaxland's book is a combination of autobiography and nature writing, but she also 'borrows' the style of another very recognisable genre for particular effect.

Key terms

convention a typical feature you find in a particular genre

intertextuality the links (direct or indirect) between individual texts

Activity 5

Though not a ghost story, Blaxland's account conjures up images of things that 'used to be' and contains words and phrases that would not be out of place in tales of horror and the supernatural. In other words, it 'borrows' conventions from another genre.

a Match the conventions below with the quotations from the text. The first one has been done for you.

Ghost story convention

A sense of mystery and uncertainty

Isolated setting

Impending sense of fear and of terrible events

Extreme weather conditions

Quotations

'One night, there was a vast electric storm of horizontal lightning, lighting up the whole barley crop as if in daylight'

'We live in a windblown house on the edge of an eroding clifftop at the easternmost end of a track which leads only into the sea'

'The Suffolk coast is eerie and deceptive'

'Then the sea will finally come, and it will devour without gratitude the ancient piece of cliff upon which the house now sits'

b Why do you think the writer uses the imagery of ghosts and horror stories? How does this contribute to the mood of the extract? Choose one of the following statements and write a paragraph to explain your choice. Some of the words from Activity 3 might be useful.

- She wants readers to appreciate the threatening power of nature.
- She wants readers to understand that the landscape, like life, is not permanent.
- She wants readers to share her own feelings of anxiety at living in such a dangerous place.

Putting it all together

Activity 6

Your feelings about a place can change depending upon the time of day/year, the people around you or even your own mood.

a Choose a place you know well, for example a local park, a particular building, a natural location or a sporting venue.

b Describe the place and create contrasting moods within your writing. Use the table below to help you. Choose one word from each column to help structure your writing.

Column A	Column B
eerie	exciting
dangerous	comforting
isolated	busy
melancholy	joyful
tranquil	ominous

Try to include some of the ghost story conventions listed on page 150.

Stretch yourself

Look back at your work on structure in previous units. How does Blaxland structure this extract to build towards a powerful conclusion? You could consider:

- the shift between descriptions of different parts of the landscape
- the shift between past and present events
- the mood created at the end of the extract.

✅ Tip

You can look back at Activity 3 to help with contrasting moods; Activity 5 to help you with genre conventions and your writing from Units 2 and 4 to help with vocabulary and figurative language.

3.7 How can we write about environmental issues?

In this unit, you will:

- learn more about rhetorical skills

- explore how to structure and present an argument

- write and present your point of view about an environmental issue.

What's the big idea?

In the last unit, you read Juliet Blaxland's description of how nature's power can impact upon the very places in which we live. However, the relationship between humans and nature is a fragile one, and in this unit, you will read an environmentalist's appeal for a more active approach to climate concerns. You will consider how a writer shapes and presents an effective argument and how they use rhetorical skills to give impact to their message. Then you will write and present your own speech using these devices.

Activity 1

a Why is it important to structure and organise your writing? What do you already know about how to do this?

b Think of **persuasive** texts that you have encountered in previous chapters (these could be fiction or non-fiction). What sort of **rhetorical devices** were used in these texts?

c Look closely at the images on this page. What do you think and feel when you look at the two images?

d Imagine you have been asked to use these images in a leaflet informing young people about climate change. How would they help to convey your message?

🔑 Key terms

persuasive making you want to do or believe something

rhetorical device a language feature that has a persuasive or impressive effect on listeners and readers

Dr Mya-Rose Craig is an ornithologist (an expert on birds), environmentalist and diversity activist as well as an author, speaker and broadcaster. In the article below, Dr Craig talks about her involvement in the Youth Strikes for Climate in September 2019 and why she feels that the movement is important.

Taking our future into our own hands

by Dr Mya-Rose Craig

1. The global climate strikes have created a pivotal cry for our world and our future. The **momentum** is gathering. We are shouting and people are starting to listen.

2. My generation is more aware of climate breakdown and the impact it will have than any generation before us and so, as a whole, we are trying to show how important the climate crisis is. […]

3. The reason we are protesting and taking part in the **Youth Strikes for Climate** boils down to the fact that our government and policymakers have not taken sufficient action to combat climate breakdown, and, like most governments around the world, are almost completely ignoring it as it does not fit in with their own agendas. The world is dominated by those making money from **plundering** it and the politicians who are benefiting from their donations and **lobbying**. Many of us have become **disenfranchised** with the system.

4. I have never seen anything like the strikes, which are energising so many people my age around the world. It has given us hope and – more importantly – motivation to act. […]

5. On Friday 20th September we asked everyone to join with us in an international strike, demanding governments around the world to take action to stop climate breakdown as it is almost too late. There are very few large impact protests like this that focus on the needs and desires of young people, giving us a voice. […]

6. I have been involved with the UK organisers and have been relentlessly speaking to people my age; asking my friends who are striking why the responses ranged from "I don't want to die before I'm fifty" to "I want to be a part of something important" to "Decisions are being made without us. It has to change."

7. Although some schools have not been happy about striking, mine has been very good. When I first asked my head of the sixth form about the consequences of striking, he only responded by saying "I can't **endorse** it" with a smile. Schools should be supporting pupils to strike as the benefits of engaging them in politics and protest far outweigh the lessons missed. [...]

8. Another reason that I care so deeply about climate breakdown is the impact it will have on people in poor countries who have not contributed to its cause and can do nothing to stop it; sixteen of the twenty countries most at risk from climate breakdown are in the developing world.

9. On Friday my home city, Bristol, had an amazing turnout of 10,000 for the protest. This was the third highest in the country. It is vital the country gets behind our young people and their demands for action on climate change, as they did on Friday, to show that we will not take no for an answer.

Youth Strikes for Climate – inspired by Greta Thunberg, these protests aimed to raise young people's awareness of the impact of climate change

lobbying – influencing politicians about an issue for one's own advantage

endorse – approve or support

⭐ Boosting your vocabulary

Skilled writers choose their words with care. The activity below explores some of the vocabulary used in the source text, which has been highlighted on page 153.

Activity 2

a   The word 'disenfranchised' means 'feeling alienated, powerless and unrepresented'. The prefix 'dis-' means 'lack of' or 'not' (for example, 'dishonest' means 'not honest'). However, just because a word begins with 'dis-' does not mean it follows this rule.

Here are some words beginning with 'dis-'. Identify which ones *do not* use 'dis-' as a prefix.

distance   disbelief   discover   disagree   disco

disaster   disease   dishcloth

b   The word 'momentum' means the ability something has to keep increasing in speed and power. Its Latin root is *movimentum*. Other words that come from this root are moment, motion, mobile and motor – they all have something to do with movement.

The words 'emotion', 'remove' and 'promote' also come from this root. Explain what you think these words might have to do with movement.

c   'Plundering' means stealing things by force. Some synonyms for plunder are 'loot', 'ransack' and 'pillage'. The word is normally associated with violent events such as rioting and war. Why do you think Dr Craig uses this word instead of 'stealing'? What does it suggest about her attitude towards the people she is describing?

Building your knowledge

In her article, Dr Craig uses a well-established framework to structure her argument. It is a structure that was outlined 2000 years ago by Marcus Tullius Cicero, who was a Roman orator (public speaker), politician and statesperson. Cicero's six-part structure is as follows:

Sections of the structure	Function
1 Introduction	Gain the attention of your audience.
2 Narration	Put your argument into context. What is the background to your argument? Who is involved?
3 Focus your message	Explain the key issues you are addressing.
4 Key points	Make your argument clear. Provide detailed support for your claim. Use both logical reasoning and factual evidence.
5 Counter-argument	Acknowledge the other side of the argument and then dismiss its claims.
6 Conclusion	Summarise your argument and inspire your audience to action.

Activity 3

Dr Craig's argument follows Cicero's structure quite closely, despite there being more than 2000 years between them.

a Complete a table like the one below. For each part of the structure, provide evidence from the text to show how Dr Craig's argument fits this framework and explain your reasoning. The first row has been completed for you.

Cicero's structure	Dr Craig's paragraph	Evidence	Explanation
1 Introduction	1	'The momentum is gathering.'	Suggests that more people are getting involved – we are not alone in our fight!
2 Narration	2		
3 Focus	3		
4 Key points	4, 5, 6, 8		
5 Counter-argument	7		
6 Conclusion	9		

b Why do you think section 4 (the key points) is the longest section?

155

Giving a speech is similar to preparing a written argument, but it requires much more than great words on a page. You also need to deliver it with confidence and with a style that engages an audience. The following are the physical aspects of talk (in other words, the presentation skills).

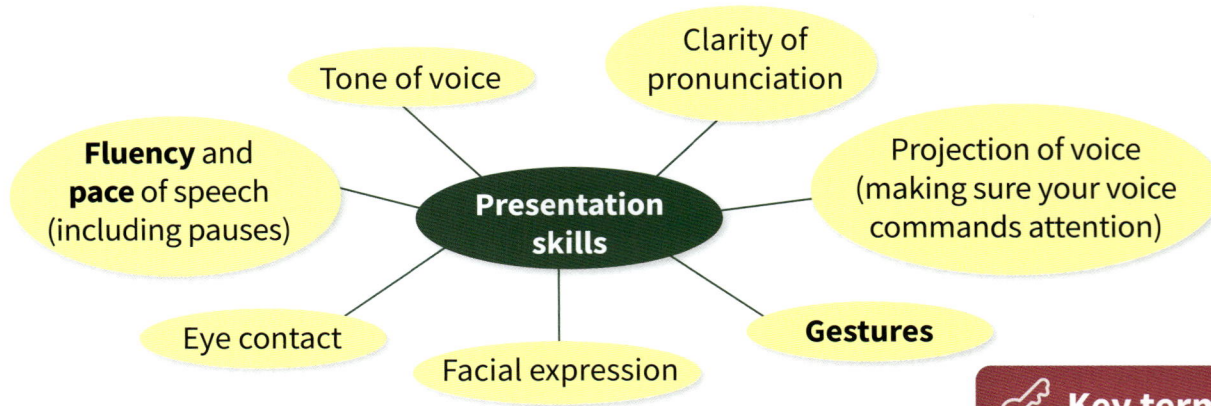

- Tone of voice
- Clarity of pronunciation
- **Fluency** and **pace** of speech (including pauses)
- **Presentation skills**
- Projection of voice (making sure your voice commands attention)
- Eye contact
- Facial expression
- **Gestures**

Key terms

fluency speaking with a smooth flow, without hesitating

gesture using your hands to indicate meaning, e.g. to help emphasise certain points

pace the speed at which someone speaks or moves or something happens

Activity 4

Look again at the first paragraph of Dr Craig's article.

Decide where you would put the following directions to help her to deliver this argument effectively:

i Emphasise these words that feel important.

ii Add physical gestures here to back up ideas.

iii Pause here for dramatic effect.

Activity 5

Look at the following extracts from the article. Try to deliver these lines in different ways to create different effects, for example anger, frustration, excitement or disbelief.

Tip

Remember to think about the physical aspects of talk, outlined above.

a 'My generation is more aware of climate breakdown and the impact it will have than any generation before us'

b 'we are trying to show how important the climate crisis is.'

c 'I have never seen anything like the strikes, which are energising so many people my age around the world. It has given us hope and – more importantly – motivation to act.'

d 'sixteen of the twenty countries most at risk from climate breakdown are in the developing world.'

Putting it all together

Activity 6

Write and present a speech giving your point of view about an environmental topic.

a Choose a topic that you feel strongly about. It could be provoked by one of the statements below.

> With more people using the Internet and staying indoors, it is time that we considered building homes on public parks.

> We should limit car ownership to one per household. This will ensure more people use public transport and bicycles.

b Plan your argument, using Cicero's six-part framework to structure your argument. You may wish to use a table like the one below.

Section of speech	What I will say...
1 Powerful opening (introduction)	
2 What has provoked my speech? (narration)	
3 What is the issue I am addressing? Why is it important? (focus)	
4 Two or three points to support my argument (key points)	
5 Why might people disagree with me? (counter-argument)	
6 Powerful ending – leave audience in no doubt that I am right! (conclusion)	

c Write your speech, following your plan.

d Practise your speech before presenting it to others. Remember to think about:

- your tone of voice and clarity of pronunciation
- the pace of delivery – including where to pause for impact
- emphasising certain words or phrases for effect
- gestures, eye contact and facial expressions.

3.8 How do writers describe future spaces?

In this unit, you will:

- learn about the subgenre of climate fiction

- understand what is meant by exposition in a narrative

- consider the ways in which a writer presents future worlds.

What's the big idea?

Over the last three units, you have read about nature's determination to thrive in the marginal spaces of our cities; of how the landscape is unpredictable and can literally disappear from beneath us; and about young people taking action to persuade those in power to focus on the environmental problems facing us all.

In this final unit, you will consider a fictional account of a future world in which many contemporary concerns about climate change and the environment are explored. You will also learn how skilled writers reveal subtle details to create the setting of their fictional worlds.

Activity 1

a   What science-fiction stories or films do you know? Do science-fiction stories have to be set in outer space or on other worlds?

b   The four statements below all describe future possibilities. Put them in order according to how likely you think they are to come true. Explain the reasons for your decisions.

All shopping will be done online and delivered by robots – there will be no need for actual shops.	We will save the polar ice caps and all natural life there will be protected.
We will run out of fossil fuel completely and all electricity will be solar- or wind-powered.	There will be no need for passports and everyone will be free to travel wherever they wish.

The extract opposite is taken from the beginning of *Exodus* by Julie Bertagna, which published in 2002. Set in 2099 on the fictional island of Wing, it describes a world where the sea levels have risen, swallowing huge portions of land and destroying whole towns and cities.

Extract from *Exodus* by Julie Bertagna

Mara Bell wakens full of restless flutterings, as if there's a tiny bird trapped in her heart.

The air is full of the noise of hammers and saws. Quickly, Mara unbolts her window and unlatches the storm shutters. Sunlight explodes into the room. She blinks, stunned and delighted, then leans out of the window and revels in the sensation of fresh air, in the panorama of sea and sky; an endless, electric blue.

Frantic activity fills the island as the people of Wing take their chance, during this rare lull in the weather, to repair the storm-battered barricades.

"Breakfast, Marabel!" her mother's clear, quick voice calls up, merging her two plain names into one beautiful sound, like water running over shoes.

[...] Mara flings on her clothes and races downstairs to escape the house she has been trapped in for three interminably long months of storm. Mara races down through the sloping field of windmills and solar panes.

Free at last! It feels glorious. The world's wind sweeps across the ocean and wraps her in billows that swirl up her dark fall of hair. The morning sun on her skin is bliss. The never-ending blue of sky and ocean is heaven to her eyes after months of dim lantern-lit light and staring at walls.

When she reaches the hump-backed road bridge where the old red telephone box sits alongside a storm-rent bus-stop sign, she pauses. Once upon a time Wing had all sorts of vehicles – buses, cars, motorbikes, lorries and tractors. Mara has seen old photographs of them. But when the fuel ran out, over half a century ago, they were all recycled for other uses. Nowadays, the only vehicle Wing ever sees is the rusted shell of a car that's sometimes swept ashore and eagerly melted down for its metal. But the islanders could not bear to recycle the metal telephone box or the bus-stop sign. They were part of the island's landscape, every bit as much as the church or the **standing stones**.

Mara feels a tremor of fear as she sees how much the ocean has risen over the winter. The hump-backed bridge runs straight into the waves. The sea can't come any closer, surely? The thought is too awful, so to put it out of her mind she runs to the edge of the waves to see what the storm has cast up.

A shoe! Mara rushes over to grab this precious bit of **flotsam** that the ocean has flung upon the grass. If she could just find *one* more. She looks down at her burst, heavily patched terrainers, hand-me-downs from her mother and grandmother. She desperately needs new shoes and doesn't care how mismatched they are.

---

standing stones – arrangements of stones dating back to ancient times (for example, Stonehenge)

flotsam – debris that has been washed ashore (often from shipwrecks)

⭐ Boosting your vocabulary

Skilled writers choose their words with care. The activity below explores some of the vocabulary used in the source text, which has been highlighted on page 159.

Activity 2

a i The word 'terrainers' is a **neologism** combining the words 'trainers' and 'terrain'. Writers may introduce neologisms to describe new objects or ideas. For example, 'webinar' comes from combining 'web' and 'seminar'. Create your own neologism by combining two familiar words.

ii The word 'terrain' means 'a stretch of land' and comes from the Latin word *terra* meaning 'earth'. Can you think of other words that derive from this word? Make a list and use them in a sentence. For example, 'extra-terrestrial' means something that is outside of the Earth's atmosphere, such as stars and other planets.

b The word 'interminably' is used to describe something that feels never-ending. Use the word in a sentence of your own.

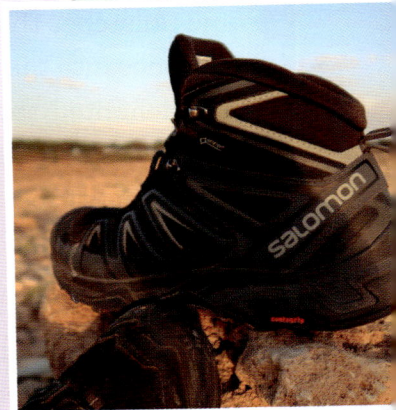

💡 Building your knowledge

Exodus belongs to a relatively new **subgenre** of science fiction called climate fiction. Writers of climate fiction address contemporary environmental concerns such as pollution or the extinction of species, and they imagine future worlds that show the negative consequences of these issues.

In climate fiction, a current environmental issue, which is irreversible, will form the basis of the story.

Other conventions of climate fiction are:

- Future Earth is often the setting or main idea. Some stories may be set on another world, perhaps because people have had to leave Earth due to climate problems.
- The future world that is described contains many recognisable characteristics of life today. However, the writer will also include elements that are unfamiliar and often disturbing.
- The stories feature recognisable characters, for example ordinary people who have to deal with the consequences of severe climate change, or scientists who can explain or try to find solutions to the problems.
- Stories include recognisable objects that will appear as relics (objects from an earlier time) in the climate-fiction world.

🗝 Key terms

exposition (in a story) background information, often giving details about what happened before the story began

inference a conclusion reached by reasoning

neologism a newly created word or expression, or a new meaning for an existing word

subgenre a subdivision of a genre, e.g. climate fiction is a subgenre of science fiction

Activity 3

a Which elements of Mara's world are recognisable to us and which tell us clearly that this is a future world? Complete a table, like the one started below, to record your ideas.

	Familiar	Unfamiliar
Weather		
Objects		
Events/characters' behaviour		

b What other conventions of climate fiction do you recognise in the extract?

Exposition is a key element in the storytelling process. It provides important background details about a particular event, setting or character to help the reader understand what is happening and why. This is especially important when describing future settings as it prevents the reader from becoming too confused by lots of new ideas.

- Exposition can be introduced slowly throughout the story. However, if too much exposition is introduced at once, it can slow down the pace of the narrative.
- Clumsy exposition tries to tell us too much information in one go. Often the information isn't relevant to the story. Good exposition shows rather than tells.
- Writers may decide to limit the amount of exposition they include in order to create anticipation, forcing the reader to make **inferences** to predict what might happen next.

Activity 4

a Consider the two attempts at exposition below. Which do you think is more successful? Explain your answer, thinking about the information in the bullet points above.

1 Sasha was a Year 8 pupil at The Tellme School in Dullsville. She had English every day of the week and her teacher was Mr Longstory. He was fairly young and had been at the school for three years. When she was in primary school, she really liked English, and her teacher, Mr Fullstop. She didn't like English any more mainly because she didn't write as many stories but also because she had to sit by Daniel, who annoyed her.

2 Sasha sighed as she walked into English.
"Are we finally going to write a story today, sir?" she asked Mr Longstory, glancing sideways at Daniel, who was picking his nose again. He had to be the most annoying Year 8 pupil ever.
"You've asked me that every lesson this week, Sasha. And the answer is no."

b How could you improve the exposition in the less successful example?

Activity 5

Writers do not *tell* their readers everything. Instead, we have to read closely, draw conclusions and make inferences about the story world from the information provided.

a   Here are some statements from the extract. What can you infer from these details? Complete a table like the one below. The first row has been done for you.

What we are told (what we can retrieve)	What the writer shows (what we have to infer)
There is no more fuel.	Fuel-powered vehicles cannot run, which is why there are no more cars.
People are frantically repairing the buildings.	
Mara hasn't been outside for three months.	
It's been dark for several months.	
A bridge is almost covered by the sea.	
Cars and shoes are swept ashore by the sea.	

b   What do you think Bertagna wants the reader to think about Mara's world and the climate issues that have created it? Why?

c   Read the statement by one reader of the book below, and answer the question.

> 'There is too much exposition in the second half of the extract. It slows down the story too much.' Do you agree with this statement? Consider:
> * which details are absolutely necessary for readers to understand the story
> * what these details tell us about Mara's world.

d   How does the writer build reader anticipation? After reading the extract, what other story details are you keen to discover?

Putting it all together

Activity 6

Read the question below.

> How has Bertagna created a convincing future world?

Refer back to your work completed earlier in this unit and then write a response. Think about:

- the description of the setting and characters
- her use of climate-fiction conventions
- the use of exposition in building the story world.

Use details from the extract to support your ideas.

You may also find some of the sentence starters below helpful.

> One way that Bertagna has created a convincing world is through the description of setting…

> Another reason that the world is convincing is because of the climate issues it addresses. One of these is…

> However, the writer also creates anticipation in the reader by withholding some information such as…

Stretch yourself

One common feature of science fiction is the use of everyday objects as relics. In *Exodus*, Bertagna reveals objects such as bus-stop signs and telephone boxes as relics. Why do you think science-fiction writers include these relics in their stories? Can you think of examples from other stories set in the future?

Key terms glossary

abbreviation a shortened form of a word or phrase

ambiguity having more than one meaning

anecdote a short or entertaining story about real people or events

antagonist main opponent

antithesis a rhetorical device that expresses opposing or contrasting ideas

antonym a word that has the opposite meaning of a particular word

archaic old-fashioned, from a different historical time

autobiography the story of a person's life, written by that person

biography the story of a person's life, written by someone else

chairperson a person who is in charge of a meeting

chronological order the order in which things happened

clause a part of a sentence with its own verb

colloquial suitable for ordinary conversation rather than formal speech or writing

colloquial language informal words or phrases that are suitable for ordinary conversation, rather than formal speech or writing

complex sentence a multi-clause sentence with at least one subordinate clause, e.g. *He stopped because he was tired.*

connotation an idea or feeling linked to a word, as well as its main meaning

context the time, place and influences on a text from when it was written, and from when it is read, which shape our understanding of the text

convention a typical feature you find in a particular genre

counter-argument an argument that opposes the point put forward

declarative a sentence that makes a statement

dialect a form of a language linked to a specific region, e.g. Geordie in Newcastle upon Tyne

direct address addressing the reader as you

direct speech the words that are actually spoken, usually presented in quotation marks

discourse marker a word or phrase that makes a link between points and organises text

editorial a newspaper article expressing a writer's opinion

emotive language word choices that create a strong emotional reaction in the audience or reader

epigram the expression of an idea in a short, memorable way

etymology a description of the origin and history of a particular word

exclamatory statement a sentence that expresses sudden or strong emotions, such as excitement. It usually ends with an exclamation mark

exposition (in a story) background information, often giving details about what happened before the story began

extended metaphor a long metaphor which builds up an image in detail over many lines

figurative language words or phrases with a meaning that is different from the literal meaning

first-person narrative a story told by someone as if they were involved in the events themselves, using first-person pronouns, e.g. *I* and *we*

fluency speaking with a smooth flow, without hesitating

foreshadowing a technique that gives a hint of something that will develop later

genre a type of story, e.g. *horror, romance, adventure, science fiction*

gesture using your hands to indicate meaning, e.g. to help emphasise certain points

homophone a word that sounds the same as another, but is spelled differently and means something different

iambic pentameter a line of poetry with five iambic 'feet'. An iambic foot is a pair of syllables: one unstressed syllable followed by a stressed one (as in 'da DUM')

imagery language that creates pictures in the reader's mind

imperative a sentence that gives an order, command or instruction

infer to work something out from what is seen, said or done, even though it is not stated directly

inference a conclusion reached by reasoning

interrogative a sentence that asks a question

intertextuality the links (direct or indirect) between individual texts

juxtapose to put words, ideas or images together to show a contrast or relationship between them

metaphor a comparison that says one thing is something else, e.g. *Amy was a rock*

modal verb a verb that works with another verb to show that something needs to happen or might possibly happen, e.g. *must, shall, will, should, would, can, could, may* and *might*

motion a statement, idea or policy that is discussed in a debate

multi-clause sentence a sentence with more than one clause, each with its own main verb, e.g. *The judge frowned and lifted her hammer.*

multimodal having or involving many methods (modes), e.g. text, images, motion, audio

narrative voice the perspective (viewpoint) from which a story is told, and the style in which it is told

narrator a person who tells a story, especially in a book, play or film

neologism a newly created word or expression, or a new meaning for an existing word

non-standard English an informal version of English, often used with family and friends, including slang and regional variations

noun phrase a noun plus information before and/or after the noun

opposition a statement that opposes a judgement or opinion

pace the speed at which someone speaks or moves or something happens

past tense a verb form that shows actions or events that have already happened

personification showing something non-human as having human characteristics

persuasive making you want to do or believe something

possessive determiner a word that comes before a noun to show whose it is, e.g. *my, your, her*

prefix a word or group of letters placed in front of another word to add to or change its meaning

present tense a verb form that describes actions which are happening now

pronoun a word used instead of a noun or noun phrase, e.g. *he, it, they*

pronunciation the sound made when a word is spoken

proposition a statement that expresses a judgement or opinion

prose written language in its ordinary form, rather than poetry or drama

quatrain a stanza of four lines, often with a strict rhythm and rhyme scheme

recount an account (written or spoken) of an event or experience

register the manner of speaking or writing, which can range between formal and informal

repetition using the same word or phrase more than once

rhetorical device a language feature that has a persuasive or impressive effect on listeners and readers

rhetorical question a question asked for dramatic effect and not intended to get an answer

rhyme using the same sound to end words, particularly at the ends of lines

rhyming couplet two consecutive lines of poetry that have rhyming final words

rhythm the pattern of beats in a line of music or poetry

Romantic era a cultural movement in the late 18th and early 19th centuries, which emphasised intense emotion and idealised the natural world

root the core of a word that has meaning. It may or may not be a complete word

sarcasm the use of humour or saying the opposite of what is meant to mock or criticise someone

second person a narrative voice that addresses the reader directly, using the pronoun *you*

setting where the action takes place

simile a comparison of one thing to another, using 'as' or 'like', e.g. *He swam like a fish*

slogan a short, catchy word or phrase used to advertise something or represent the aims of a campaign or organisation

sonnet a short poetic form, typically of 14 lines with ten syllables per line

Standard English a widely recognised formal version of English, not linked to any region, but used in schools, exams, official publications and in public announcements

subgenre a subdivision of a genre, e.g. climate fiction is a subgenre of science fiction

subvert to change an established way something is done

summarise to give the key points

superlative the form of an adjective or adverb that means 'most'

suspense a feeling of anxious uncertainty while waiting for something to happen or become known

symbol something specific that represents a more general quality or situation

synonym a word or phrase that means the same, or almost the same, as another word or phrase

tension a feeling of being on edge with nerves stretched tight

the floor the formal term to describe everyone participating in a debate apart from the chairperson and main speakers

the media all means of communicating with a large audience through various outlets, such as television broadcasting, advertising, newspapers and the Internet

the supernatural events and forces that cannot be explained by the known laws of nature or science

third person a narrative voice that informs the reader of what is taking place, using the pronouns *he, she* or *they*

This house believes… a formal way of introducing a motion

tone the speaker's or writer's feeling or attitude expressed towards their subject

tricolon a pattern of three words or phrases grouped together to be memorable and have impact

Boosting your vocabulary glossary

acquainted *(verb)* known someone slightly

adhered *(verb)* stuck to something

advert *(noun)* an advertisement; a public notice or announcement, especially one advertising goods or services in newspapers, on posters or in broadcasts

afar *(adjective)* far away

ancient *(adjective)* very old

appease *(verb)* to calm someone down, often by giving them what they want

aspect *(noun)* a person's or thing's appearance

assertive *(adjective)* acting forcefully and with confidence

audit *(verb)* to officially examine or check something for its accuracy

bark *(noun) (old use)* a small ship

bidding *(verb)* commanding someone to do something

collaborated *(verb)* worked together on a job

credible *(adjective)* able to be believed; convincing

creed *(noun)* belief or set of beliefs in something

darkling *(adjective)* increasingly dark

deceptive *(adjective)* not what it seems to be; giving a false impression

democracy *(noun)* government of a country by representatives elected by all the people

desolate *(adjective)* lonely and sad

devour *(verb)* to eat or swallow something hungrily or greedily

discover *(verb)* to find or find out something, especially by searching

disenfranchised *(adjective)* with rights taken away, especially a right to vote

dispose *(verb)* to dispose of something is to get rid of it

doomed *(adjective)* certain to suffer a grim fate

dousing *(verb)* pouring water or other liquid over something

embodiment *(noun)* the expression of principles or ideas in a visible form

escapism *(noun)* escaping from the difficulties of life by thinking about or doing more pleasant things

ferreting *(verb)* searching or rummaging about for something

force *(noun)* strength or power

frequented *(verb)* visited a place or was seen there, often

generation *(noun)* all the people born at about the same time

imminent *(adjective)* likely to happen at any moment

implications *(noun)* possible effects or results of something

inconsequential *(adjective)* of no consequence; unimportant

incorporating *(verb)* including something as a part of something larger

insidious *(adjective)* causing harm gradually without being noticed

inspiring *(adjective)* filling a person with ideas, enthusiasm or creative feeling

integrity *(noun)* being honest and behaving well

interminably *(adverb)* seeming to go on for ever; long and boring

invest *(verb)* to give time or money to a particular purpose or cause, with the expectation that it will be beneficial

just *(adjective)* fair and right; giving proper consideration to everyone's claims

manually *(adverb)* worked by or done with the hands

masquerade *(noun)* a type of party where people wear costumes and masks over their faces, to hide their identities

mesmerising *(adjective)* fascinating or able to hold a person's attention

momentum *(noun)* the ability something has to keep developing or increasing

monitor *(verb)* to regularly watch or test what is happening with something

observing *(verb)* seeing and noticing something

oft *(adverb) (old use)* often

omnipresent *(adjective)* present everywhere

plundering *(verb)* robbing a person or place using force, especially during a war

principal *(adjective)* chief or most important

progress *(noun)* development or improvement

prosperity *(noun)* being successful or rich

purged *(adjective)* rid of unwanted people or things

revenge *(verb)* to harm someone in return for harm that they have done to you

satiating *(verb)* satisfying an appetite or desire fully

sinister *(adjective)* wicked; intending to do harm

spectral *(adjective)* ghostly

sporadic *(adjective)* happening or found at irregular intervals; scattered

stagnant *(adjective)* not flowing

strident *(adjective)* loud and harsh

suffocating *(verb)* making it difficult or impossible for someone to breathe

supervise *(verb)* to be in charge of a person or thing and inspect what is done

supervising *(verb)* being in charge of a person or thing and inspecting what is done

terrainers *(noun)* a neologism combining the words 'trainers' and 'terrain'

transition *(noun)* the process of changing from one state or form to another

unique *(adjective)* being the only one of its kind; unlike any other

unromantic *(adjective)* not romantic; not to do with love or romance

vigorous *(adjective)* full of strength and energy

wavering *(adjective)* being unsteady or moving unsteadily

OXFORD
UNIVERSITY PRESS

Great Clarendon Street, Oxford, OX2 6DP, United Kingdom

Oxford University Press is a department of the University of Oxford. It furthers the University's objective of excellence in research, scholarship, and education by publishing worldwide. Oxford is a registered trade mark of Oxford University Press in the UK and in certain other countries.

© Oxford University Press 2023

The moral rights of the authors have been asserted

First published in 2023

All rights reserved. No part of this publication may be reproduced, stored in a retrieval system, or transmitted, in any form or by any means, without the prior permission in writing of Oxford University Press, or as expressly permitted by law, by licence or under terms agreed with the appropriate reprographics rights organization. Enquiries concerning reproduction outside the scope of the above should be sent to the Rights Department, Oxford University Press, at the address above.

You must not circulate this work in any other form and you must impose this same condition on any acquirer

British Library Cataloguing in Publication Data
Data available

978-138-203331-2

978-138-203332-9 (ebook)

10 9 8 7 6 5 4 3 2 1

Paper used in the production of this book is a natural, recyclable product made from wood grown in sustainable forests.

The manufacturing process conforms to the environmental regulations of the country of origin.

Printed in China by Shanghai Offset Printing Products Ltd.

Acknowledgements

The publisher would like to thank the following for permissions to use their copyrighted material:

Julie Bertagna: Extract from *Exodus* by Julie Bertagna, published by Macmillan Children's Books. Reprinted by permission of David Higham Associates

Brian Bilston: 'Make Poetry Not War' by Brian Bilston © Brian Bilston. Reproduced with permission of Jo Unwin Literary Agency Ltd

Malorie Blackman: Extract adapted from Malorie Blackman's novel by Dominic Cooke, *Noughts & Crosses*, 2008. Reproduced with permission of Oxford University Press through PLSclear

Juliet Blaxland: Extract from *The Easternmost House* by Juliet Blaxland. Copyright © Juliet Blaxland 2018. Reproduced by permission of Sandstone Press Ltd.

Dr Mya-Rose Craig: Extract from 'Taking our future into our own hands' by Dr Mya-Rose Craig. Reproduced by permission of Dr Mya-Rose Craig

Green Teenager: Extract from 'Best Teenager Influencers: 15 Teen Sensations You Must Follow on Social Media' by Bonita Brown, 15 November 2019. Reproduced with permission of Green Teenager

Guardian: Extract from 'Video games can improve mental health. Let's stop seeing them as a guilty pleasure' by Keza MacDonald, 23 November 2020. Reproduced with permission of Guardian News & Media Limited

Guardian: Extract from 'The Dartmoor wild camping ban futher limits our right to roam. It must be fought' by Sophie Pavelle, 17 January 2023. Reproduced with permission of Guardian News & Media Limited

Mariette Lindstein: Extract from *Fog Island*, reprinted by permission of HarperCollins Publishers Ltd © 2019 Mariette Lindstein

Nicholas Lloyd: Extract from 'Meet the one-eyed robot - it's fantastic', Daily Herald, 16 Oct 1958, reprinted by permission of Mirrorpix, for Trinity Mirror Publishing Ltd.

Stephenie Meyer: Excerpts from *Twilight* by Stephenie Meyer © 2005 Stephenie Meyer. Reproduced with permission of Little Brown Book Group Limited through PLSclear

Mary McIntyre: Extract from 'An astronomer's guide to stargazing with the naked eye', reproduced with permission of Mary McIntyre and CPRE The countryside charity

MIT News: Extract from 'Helping companies deploy AI models more responsibly' by Zach Winn, 10 February 2023. Used with permission of Massachusetts Institute of Technology News Office

Sara Maitland: Extract from *A Book Of Silence* by Sara Maitland, published by Granta Books. Reprinted by permission of Granta Books

Patrick Ness: Extract from *A Monster Calls* by Patrick Ness. Text © 2011 Patrick Ness from an original idea by Siobhan Dowd. Reproduced by permission of Walker Books Ltd, London www.walker.co.uk

Tahereh Mafi: Extract from *An Emotion of Great Delight* reprinted by permission of HarperCollins Publishers Ltd © 2021 Tahereh Mafi

Richard Mabey: Extract from *The Unofficial Countryside* by Richard Mabey. Copyright © Richard Mabey 1973. Reproduced by permission of Sheil Land Associates Ltd

Sam Selvon: Extract from *The Lonely Londoners* reprinted with permission of Susheila Nasta on behalf of the Estate of Sam Selvon

Greta Thunberg: Extract from 'Can you Hear Me?' Houses of Parliament, London 23 April 2019 from *No One Is Too Small to Make a Difference* by Greta Thunberg published by Penguin. Copyright © Greta Thunberg, 2019. Reprinted by permission of Penguin Books Limited.

Photos: p8(1): Ink Drop/Shutterstock; **p8(2):** Photo Kozyr/Shutterstock; **p9(3):** Elizabeth A.Cummings/Shutterstock; **p9(4):** Monkey Business Images/Shutterstock; **p9(5):** Chay_Tee/Shutterstock; **p9(6):** Vasin Lee/Shutterstock; **p12:** Everett Collection/ Shutterstock; **p13(bkg):** REDPIXEL.PL/Shutterstock; **p14:** Joseph Sohm/Shutterstock; **p16:** DGLimages / Shutterstock; **pp18-19:** 1000 Words/Shutterstock; **pp20-21:** Sipa US / Alamy Stock Photo; **p22:** nicostock/Shutterstock; **pp24-25:** pxl.store / Shutterstock; **p26:** Andrea Raffin / Shutterstock; **p28:** Rawpixel.com/Shutterstock; **pp30-31:** supawat bursuk/Shutterstock; **p33:** Dan Henson / Shutterstock; **p34:** urbanbuzz / Alamy Stock Photo; **pp36-37:** Predrag Lukic/Shutterstock; **pp38-39:** alphaspirit.it/Shutterstock; **p41:** EFKS/Shutterstock; **p42:** antoniodiaz/Shutterstock; **p43:** Sakemomo/Shutterstock; **p45:** BONDART PHOTOGRAPHY/Shutterstock; **p47:** Andy119 / Shutterstock; **p48:** Travers Lewis/Shutterstock; **p49(l):** Contains public sector information licensed under the Open Government Licence v3.0.; **p49(r):** World History Archive / Alamy Stock Photo; **p50:** Arndt Sven-Erik / Arterra Picture Library / Alamy Stock Photo; **p51(i):** shadowalice / Shutterstock; **p51(ii):** Kaspri / Shutterstock; **p51(iii):** Runrun2 / Shutterstock; **p51(iv):** MF production / Shutterstock; **p51(v):** Artur Ch / Shutterstock; **p52:** Merseyside Police; **p55:** LightField Studios / Shutterstock; **p55(bkg):** Vladitto/Shutterstock; **p56:** Arnav Pratap Singh / Shutterstock; **p58:** RaiDztor/Shutterstock; **p60(1):** Den Rozhnovsky/Shutterstock; **p60(2):** SWKStock/Shutterstock; **p60(3):** Mauricio Graiki/Shutterstock; **p60(4):** Laura Crazy/ Shutterstock; **pp60-61(5):** mRGB/Shutterstock; **p60(6):** VIAVAL TOURS/Shutterstock; **p64:** Melkor3D / Shutterstock; **p66:** Roman Sigaev / Shutterstock; **p68:** Lucian BOLCA / Shutterstock; **pp70-71:** Gregory A. Pozhvanov / Shutterstock; **p72:** Roxana Bashyrova/Shutterstock; **p74:** Mimadeo / Shutterstock; **p77:** Krivosheev Vitaly / Shutterstock; **p79:** Maks Ershov / Shutterstock; **pp80-81:** rmartinr / Shutterstock; **p82:** Raggedstone/Shutterstock; **p85:** giuseppe masci / Alamy Stock Photo; **p86:** Eric Isselee / Shutterstock; **pp88-89:** Alex Mit/Shutterstock; **p91:** AstroStar/Shutterstock; **p93:** CnApTaK/Shutterstock; **p94(t):** Boris Medvedev/Shutterstock; **p94(b):** Stokkete/ Shutterstock; **p97:** VDWI Automotive / Alamy Stock Photo; **p98:** P Cox / Alamy Stock Photo; **p101:** Rawpixel.com/Shutterstock; **101(bkg):** lakshmipathilucky / Shutterstock; **p102:** TippaPatt/Shutterstock; **p104:** gg_tsukahara/Shutterstock; **p106:** Alpha Historica / Alamy Stock Photo; **p107:** Artsiom P/Shutterstock; **p109:** Zhukova Valentyna/Shutterstock; **p111:** Artsiom / Shutterstock; **p112(1):** Panikhin Sergey/ Shutterstock; **p112(2):** Martin Capek/Shutterstock; **p113(3):** fuyu liu/Shutterstock; **p113(4):** Mica Stock/Shutterstock; **p113(5):** Artic_photo/Shutterstock; **p113(6):** Photo Art Wall Decoration/Shutterstock; **p116(l):** Walker Art Library / Alamy Stock Photo; **p116(r):** Lordprice Collection / Alamy Stock Photo; **p119:** Dave Head / Shutterstock; **pp120-121:** Kevin Eaves/Shutterstock; **p123:** S.Castelli/Shutterstock; **p124:** sjbooks / Alamy Stock Photo; **p126:** TokyoVideoStock/Shutterstock; **p127(l):** Luciano Mortula - LGM / Shutterstock; **p127(r):** leshiy985 / Shutterstock; **p128:** Alexander Chizhenok / Shutterstock; **p130:** tomertu / Shutterstock; **pp132-133:** DanieleGay / Shutterstock; **pp134-135:** hanif66/Shutterstock; **p137:** Jarek Pawlak / Shutterstock; **p138:** Stefan Rotter / Shutterstock; **p140:** Andrew Parker/Alamy Stock Photo; **p142:** everydoghasastory / Shutterstock; **p144:** Abdul_Shakoor / Shutterstock; **pp146-147:** Baronb / Shutterstock; **p149:** andyrogers23 / Shutterstock; **p152(l):** TR STOK / Shutterstock; **p152(r):** DisobeyArt / Shutterstock; **p154:** Anastasiia Tymoshenko / Shutterstock; **p157:** View Apart / Shutterstock; **pp158-159:** Luma creative / Shutterstock; **p160:** Zakariaa El Mikdam / Shutterstock; **p163:** M G Photography / Shutterstock.

Artwork by Michael Driver and Geraldine Sy.

Although we have made every effort to trace and contact all copyright holders before publication this has not been possible in all cases. If notified, the publisher will rectify any errors or omissions at the earliest opportunity.

Links to third party websites are provided by Oxford in good faith and for information only. Oxford disclaims any responsibility for the materials contained in any third party website referenced in this work.